What If I'm Wrong

The Atheist's Nightmare

Ron Warren

(former Atheist)

What If I'm Wrong?

TORAHLIFE MNISTRIES, INC
851 North State Road 434, Suite 1070-178,
Altamonte Springs, Fl. 32714

Published by EA Books Publishing a division of
Living Parables of Central Florida, Inc. a 501c3
EABooksPublishing.com

DISCLAIMER

This book is designed to provide information about the subject matter covered. It is sold with the understanding that the publisher and author are not engaged in rendering legal, accounting, or professional services. If legal or other expert assistance is required, the services of a professional should be sought.

It is not the purpose of this manual to reprint all the information that is otherwise available to other authors, but to complement, amplify, and supplement other texts.

The purpose of this manual is to educate. The Author and Torahlife Ministries, Inc. shall have no liability or responsibility to any person or entity with respect to loss or damage caused or alleged to be caused by the information contained in this book.

DEDICATION

This book is dedicated to my loving wife, JoAnn, who stayed with me, even during the time that her faith had to withstand the attacks from her atheist husband. Through all the struggles, she still gave love, forgiveness, and acceptance. She is God's miracle given to me to make my life complete.

It is also dedicated to our two loving sons, Robert and Christopher, who lived through the effects.

Only in Heaven will I love you guys more.

Finally, and most important, it is dedicated to Adonai. As the "God of the Second Chance," He continually applies His grace towards me. This book was written in thanksgiving of that wonderful grace.

FOREWORD

There are times when I've watched a cooking program on television and wished there was the capability of having a smell option. I want to get the full impact of what I'm being presented. That should be the desire of every reader of this book. Those who know Ron Warren understand exactly what I'm saying! As I was reading his work, I could actually hear the power and enthusiasm of conviction of Ron's voice in every paragraph – and it made me smile!

To say that Ron has a passion for reading and teaching God's Word, is a definite understatement. When asked a one-sentence biblical question, Ron can never give a one-sentence answer. His desire is to always provide complete Scriptural understanding.

This book is a great example of Ron wanting atheists to have a clear and comprehensive understanding of the ramifications based on the decisions they have made. The extensive breath of information he provides does just that - he gives the believer the tools to successfully interact with atheists. This work is also an outstanding resource to strengthen the faith of believers.

As I read this book, Ron masterfully answered many of my long-held who, what, where when and why questions.

My personal faith is stronger as a result of facts shared and illustrations given.

So why did Ron choose to write this book? He had to. As a former atheist, Ron knows the personal pain caused by atheism and he doesn't want anyone to experience the nightmare he and his family endured.

While an atheist may never choose to read this book, I encourage every believer to not only read it but to keep it as a reference for that time or times your path will cross with someone with whom you'll be able to share based on the questions you'll know to ask.

Mark J. Goldstein, President,
Central Florida Christian Chamber of Commerce.

TESTIMONIALS

"In his book, 'What if I'm Wrong? The Atheist's Nightmare,' Ron Warren recounts his very chilling and very personal journey to discover who God really is. He recounts his journey in very succinct terms as he shares his own battle to overcome Atheism. Ron demonstrates that he is a serious seeker of truth as he peels back layer by layer the illusions of Atheism and one by one deals with every excuse embraced by the Atheist to validate their beliefs.

Ron offers irrefutable documentation that destroys each of the Atheist's arguments against the creator God, This is accomplished through rational discovery backed by a thorough understanding of how the God of the universe has revealed himself through history and Scripture.

This book is written for anyone who has a serious and honest desire to know if there is a God. Be careful as you read it, it may well change your life!"

Larry R Davis, President of Internet Revenue Specialist, and fellow searcher to know the one true God.

"A veritable feast of meat and details. It encompasses everything a Believer would need to lovingly and gently reveal the light to anyone lost in the book, 'What if I'm Wrong? The Atheist's Nightmare.' It is a ray of hope that transcends pop-evangelism and pierces through to the heart of the matter in clear and concise concepts with verifiable proofs. A beginner can read through this book and get all they need to support and defend their fledgling faith, and a battle-worn, spiritual warrior can find all the tools and encouragement necessary to press on victoriously – to the truth."

Steve Buck, The Buck Ranch

"What a marvelous roller coaster this book is. It is not just a book, it is a manual, a guidebook, a playbook, a strategy guide, and most appropriately it is a case file assembled and ready for battle in court. It was an honor to read and review Ron's book"

"'*What if I'm Wrong? The Atheist's Nightmare*' is a book that will arm every believer for trial and battle. With the growing rise of apathy and rejection of God, it is imperative that young believers read this book, absorb its contents, and prepare for battle. As a believer, it also strengthened my own faith to see scientific and historical facts lining up one right after the other, all leading towards the one truth-Yeshua our Messiah. Ron's obedience to the Lord's guidance is a blessing to all who find this book in their hands."

Vanessa Romay,
Admissions Counselor, Worship Leader

"I often like to watch science documentaries; the ones about astronomy and physics are particularly interesting. They often have nice music and eye-catching animations, even though they get the physics wrong. However, I've noticed a pattern in them. The scientist hosts of these shows almost always have to make the following declarations:

1) There is no god.

2) Those who believe in any god are stupid (or less evolved).

3) Belief in any god inhibits the science.

Ron's Book. '*What if I'm Wrong? The Atheist's Nightmare,*' destroys these declarations.

As I'm reading Ron's book, my son comes to me to tell me about a game he's playing where you colonize planets. He says to me, "Why are they having you land on Jupiter and Saturn? Don't these game designers know those planets don't have surfaces you can land on?" Then he asks, "Why did God create planets that couldn't be lived on anyway?" My answer: "In God's sovereignty, wisdom and purpose, he created those planets that way. We may not understand His why. He created them for His glory, and it's possible He created them for the express purpose to protect us on the Earth." Go back and read the 1st sentence of this paragraph. Was that a coincidence? There, God glorified in the majestic and the mundane. **Ron's book drives that point home."**

Robert Hosler, IT Specialist,
Salem Media Group

"… It Speaks! Brilliant! Spectacular! A thunderous, explosive, insightful journey into TRUTH through embedded FAITH. - A marriage between science and scripture, man and God!"

Jose Perezcassar, MD, FAAFP (Retired)

"Ron Warren is a modern-day Paul of Tarsus. Like Paul, Ron used to persecute Christians. Like Paul, Ron had an undeniable encounter with the Risen Christ. And like Paul, Ron now passionately speaks and writes about his Savior and Lord. Fasten your seatbelts, folks. Ron Warren has something to say--and it's worth hearing!"

Dawn Whitestone,
founder, Whitestone Professionals

"Triple Threat Star! He could run, throw and kick at a professional football player's level. I was awed by these types of individuals during my teen age years in the 50's.

When I became a Christian in my 30's, I began to search for an individual who was a teacher at a professional level who knew both the Old and New Testament in depth. But there was one element I overlooked until recently.

How does one effectively carry on a conversation with a die-hard unbeliever whether they are an Atheist or Agnostic while keeping one's emotions under control? The solution was revealed to me while reading Ron Warren's new book, *"What if I'm Wrong? The Atheist's Nightmare"*

This book also revealed my ignorance of the necessity to discuss a person's need for God at their level. The book also strengthened the need to follow Peter's injunction: *"but sanctify Christ as Lord in your hearts, always being ready to make a defense to everyone who asks you to give an account for the hope that is in you, yet with gentleness and reverence"* (1 Peter 3:15).

Ron Warren certainly is the person to present material from the Old Testament, New Testament and Atheism from an expert point of view because of his knowledge and experience as a Christian from his early years when he immersed himself in the scriptures; as a Messianic Minister and formerly an Atheist.

Ron certainly has attained a proficiency to present the reasons for one's beliefs as a Christian when discussing the complete Bible as one, what no matter what they believe.

This latest book by Ron Warren is a must for those who want to be ready to defend the faith under any condition.

Greg Martin, Bible and
Goyim Messianic Roots Teacher

"Reading Ron's book *'What if I'm Wrong? The Atheist's Nightmare,'* was eye-opening. Starting with the four killer questions, the book methodically presents the truth through many powerful documented resources. Ron shows and presents GOD'S perfect #7 so intricately woven through humanity and all HIS creation.

Through the modern discovery of DNA, it shows how precise our CREATOR is in HIS creation. As Sargent Friday on Dragnet used to say, "Just show me the facts," Ron has presented the facts of our CREATOR and Jesus being GOD in the flesh on earth. This parallels HIS creating earthly miracles while HE walked the earth.

Ron also supplies the ten top reasons to believe in the CREATOR AS GOD. As you read this book, you will be changed seeing how much work our GOD has put into HIS creation because HE loves us and wants us to get to know HIM better.

Blessings, and enjoy this reading adventure!"

John Grady Jr.
America's Working Class Foundation,
Homeless/Prison Ministry

SPECIAL THANKS

These people and Organizations deserve a special thank you. They wanted the book released so much that they helped overwrite the cost of the production.

Nadine Trombacco	Groveland, FL
Mark Goldstein	Apopka, FL
Dawn Whitestone	Orlando FL
The Palette	Stanford, FL
Love Missions. Org	Stanford, FL
Gregory Martin	Dover DE
Internet Revenue Specialists	Orlando FL
Alta & Larry Davis	Orlando FL
Jose Parezcassar	Winter Garden, FL
Wendy & Robert Hosler	Apopka, FL
Connie Dunn	Orlando FL
Ana & Pablo Jicueroa	Orlando FL
Steven McCarthy	Dryden, MI
Ruth & John Grady Jr.	Pensacola, FL
Elaine Howard	Winter Garden, FL
Fred Stanley	Winter Springs, FL
Grady Phillips	Lake Lure, NC
Kenneth Webb	Pensacola, FL
Kingdom Life Ministries	Chesapeake, VA
Lazarus & Maria Alvarez	Kissimmee, FL
Latin Harvest Ministries	Kissimmee, FL
Carmen L Silva	Orlando. FL
Patricia Placide	Orlando, FL
Don Cain	Orlando, FL
Stacey Forget	Orlando, FL

CONTENTS

PREFACE (My Testimony)

Faith is embedded in trust. Without trust, faith cannot exist. Such is the life of an Atheist. I can divide my testimony into two sections: the Atheist Period and the Messianic Judaism Period.

From age five until I finished eighth grade I had two hours of religious teaching a day, one hour for the Bible and one hour of church history. At five days a week and 42 weeks a year, that's a total of eight years.

By age 11, I had already outlined the entire Bible. This is my background.

In 1967, at the age of 24, I used the G.I. Bill to prepare to study for the ministry. I was going to be a Lutheran Missouri Synod minister.

A major tragedy hit me in 1969. My cousin Pauline and her five-year-old son died in a fire. Their bodies were burned so badly that they were buried together in one coffin.

At the funeral, Pauline's older brother asked me, "Why would God take the life of a five-year-old kid?" I could not answer him. The process of trying to answer that question, created more questions. Faith in God hit a roadblock. This became a turning point in my life and I decided, much to my anger, that the teaching on the resurrection was a lie.

This turned me into an atheist. God did not exist! Though I kept my change secret, I believed I had to convince everyone else—starting with my wife. I tried to use my knowledge of the Bible and history to destroy her faith in God. It was not a frontal attack but guerrilla warfare—subtle questions meant to sow doubt. Eventually she figured me out and stopped discussing her faith with me.

So I went after others. Remember, I knew church history and the start of many major doctrines. When someone wanted to discuss faith, not knowing my atheism, my sneak attack hinged on the answer to one question: "What denomination are you?" Then I would take their Bible, knowing their doctrines and its history, and start interrogating. My purpose was to make them doubt.

Most people can explain what they believe, but very few can explain why they believe it. The "what" covers the knowledge; the "how" covers the process, but the "why" covers their purpose. My questions would attack the "why" of their faith. I did this from 1969 to Resurrection Sunday morning in 1979. Then God stepped into my life through a radio program.

I had always told my wife that I would take her and our sons to church on Easter and Christmas. "For the rest of the year, do not push me." I awoke early Easter morning in a foul mood.

We had just moved from Illinois to Florida within a week. We had an apartment, but most of our things were still boxed. I had connected the stereo the night before, but found that the cord that controlled the tuner had broken during the move. I could not change the station.

At 5 a.m., I turned on the radio. It tuned to Orlando's WAJL ("We Acclaim Jesus Lord"). The man on the radio stated that he was going to prove conclusively that Jesus (Yeshua) rose from the dead. I lost it!

What happened over the next 25 minutes read like the script of a surreal sitcom. I started screaming questions at the radio. The announcer would calmly repeat my question verbatim. He then proceeded to answer, not with scripture or science but with legal arguments, as if in a court of law. This process continued for a full 25 minutes before I realized I was arguing with a radio. At the end of the program, the announcer said something that I never forgot.

"Today the scepter is in your hand. You have the right to choose. What are you going to do with Jesus? Tomorrow that scepter will be in his hands and the question will be asked, 'What will I do with you?' Today the choice is yours.

God will honor the choice you choose. Tomorrow there will be no choice. You have made it. What do you choose?"

I have just had all my questions answered on the Resurrection. I realized that for ten years I had been wrong. I also realized what I did to the faith of other people, including my wife, during those ten years. I made my choice–I will follow God until the day I die.

True story: I tried to find out who was on that radio program but could not. I was arguing with a tape over three weeks old. The station had aired it to cover that time spot and then destroyed it.

Major problem: my wife did not believe I had changed. She took over a year to accept it. I had to rebuild the trust that I'd destroyed.

When my wife returned from Israel in November 1991, she started doing "Jewish things". Being trained in Lutheran theology, it struck against every fiber of my being. A "holy jihad" hit our house lasting the full year of 1992 into April 1993, and I led the charge.

In April, we met a married couple, members of a Messianic Jewish congregation, in a grocery store. The women connected almost instantly. They invited us to come to their services. My wife accepted, and to keep peace I agreed.

My atheist mindset returned with determination to destroy this "new doctrine". The more I attacked the Rabbi with questions, the more the problems in Scripture disappeared. He was answering them from a Jewish context.

I still could not handle those "Jewish things" and started to make plans to divorce her. The lease was signed on an apartment with a woman for a roommate. I planned to leave her on November 1, 1993.

October's last week was the anniversary of this Messianic synagogue, and celebrated in Daytona Beach. Knowing what would happen on November 1, I went with my wife, our last act together, to this celebration. Again, God moved to stop me, but not in a normal way.

My wife wanted us to go through baptism. On October 31, 1993, to please my wife, I agreed. A major thing happened coming up out of that water. Remember the training I had on the Bible?

I could quote entire chapters and books before this "watershed experience." Now, I could not quote John 3:16, coming up from the water. I thought this would never happen. I still remembered the church history, but my Bible study and knowledge had disappeared - GONE! IT DID NOT MAKE SENSE! I went into a state of panic. I could not explain why it happened; I freaked, and wanted it back.

Question: When you are reading a book where do you start? Answer: At the beginning. I started to re-study the word of God with a passion. I read the first five books in Scripture non-stop two times. I developed an outline, and, for the third time, re-read the first five books, checking the outline. I finished with the rest of the Old Testament (Tanakh).

Again I re-read the entire Old Testament (Tanakh). When finished, I read the New Testament (Brit Hadashah). My mind exploded! Everything made sense from the Jewish context in the Old Testament. I studied the ancient Jewish customs, culture and history. This context showed some differences in some church doctrines.

I never divorced my wife. I canceled the lease, and took the financial loss. We are still together and love each other very much.

But in our marriage, a question remained. How do I make up for all the times I tried to destroy my wife's faith? Will I ever be able to reclaim her trust?

From 1979 to 2005 (26 years), I taught and preached in both churches and Messianic synagogues. Between the years of 2002 to 2004 I was the spiritual leader of a Messianic synagogue called B'nai Adonai ("Children of God"). During that entire time, I still had problems accepting what I had done to other people's faith, especially my wife's. My past was always before me.

In early 2005, my wife and I went to a marriage retreat in Tampa. The goal of the retreat was to strengthen and rebuild our marriages. Every time a bell would ring, we were to kiss our spouses. It was great. Then a problem occurred.

At the end of the retreat, the rabbi said that if anyone would want to be remarried, he would do it. I was not going to do it. I could not ask my wife. I was afraid and did not want to hear the rejection. I looked at my wife to tell her we were going to leave when she looked at me, tears in her eyes, and said only one word: "Please!"

With that one word, I experienced love, forgiveness, redemption, and acceptance. We were remarried and my life truly changed. On the way back from Tampa, we buried our past at the first rest stop. From that point, we never mentioned it again in anger. We had a fresh new start.

God is the God of the second chance. No one understands that better than an EX-atheist.

What If I'm Wrong

The Atheist's Nightmare

Ron Warren

(former Atheist)

FOUR KILLER QUESTIONS

These four *"Killer Questions"* are for the believer to use as he/she talks to the atheist.

1. What do you mean by that? In other words, define your terms

2. Where do you get your information?

3. How do you know that's true?

4. What if you're wrong?

The design of these questions is to make the atheist think critically about his/her beliefs. Remember, one of your challenges will be to use the right question at the right time.

Question #1: What do you mean by that?

Here you want to get the other person to define his terms and explain what he is saying. Otherwise you could end up having a conversation using the same words but meaning very different things.

Get the other person's definition. Suppose your neighbor says, "I don't believe there is a God." If you respond with "Oh, yes there is," you could quickly descend into *is-not* versus *is-too*. That's just a quarrel. 2 Timothy 2:24-25 says not to quarrel with anyone.

Instead, just start asking questions. "What do you mean by *God*? What's your understanding of this God who isn't there?" Let him define that which does not exist!

You may well find out that the god he rejects is a mean, cold, abusive overlord who looks a lot like his father. In that case, you can assure him that you don't believe in that god either. The true God is different. At this point, do not pursue the existence of God argument, but rather try to understand where he is coming from. Show the compassion and grace of God to someone bearing painful scars on his soul.

If someone says she is for a woman's right to choose abortion, you can ask, "What do you mean by *woman*? Only an adult woman? What if the baby is a girl, what about her right to choose? What do you mean by *right*? Where does that right come from?"

Asking "What do you mean by that?" can expose problems in the other person's perspective.

Question #2: Where do you get your information?

This question is particularly important in today's culture, where we drown in information from a huge array of sources. Information pumps out at us from TV, radio, music, Websites, email, blogs, billboards, movies, and conversations with people who have no truth filters in place at all. Consider the kind of responses you could get to the question, "Where do you get your information?"

"I heard it somewhere." Well, how's that for reliable? Follow with another killer question, "How do you know it's true?"

"Everybody says so." That may be so, but is it true? If you repeat a lie loud enough, often enough, and long enough, people will believe it.

For example, "everybody says" gay people are born that way. Doesn't everybody know that by now? That's what we hear every day, but where is the science to back up that assertion? Nowhere, it turns out. Not a shred of proof for a gay gene.

Someone else may say, "I read it somewhere." So ask where? Is it a legitimate newspaper or magazine? Or a tabloid? You might have read that Elvis is alive or that you can lose 25 pounds in a week, but there is a word for that kind of writing: fiction.

Did you see it on the Web? That could be an individual blogger posting total fabrication as fact, and great computer graphics can make complete fantasy look real. Or it could be a trustworthy, legitimate Website like Probe.org that makes its sources and mission clear to all.

Did you see it on TV? Who said it, and how trustworthy is the source? Was it fact or opinion? Be aware of the agenda behind the major media outlets. Former CBS reporter Bernard Goldberg exposed the leftist leanings of the media in his book *Bias: A CBS Insider Exposes How the Media Distort the News*. Because of what you see on TV is "flawed" we are to be discerning and skeptical of the values and information it pumps out.

Don't be fooled by people sounding confident and self-assured. They may not have any basis for feeling that way.

Question #3: How do you know that's true?

This is probably the most powerful question of them all. It puts the burden of proof on the other person.

Most people aren't aware of what they merely assume to be true; they simply have no other way to see the world. They often believe what they believe without asking why. If you respectfully ask, "How do you know that's true?" folks can start to realize that what they believe is by faith. But where do they place their faith?

Sometimes, the kindest thing you can do for people is gently shake up their presuppositions and invite them to think.

Many scientists believe in other dimensions or universes even though they cannot be observed or measured; but the reigning philosophy for many today is materialism, the insistence that the physical universe is all that exists. Something is only real if you can measure and quantify it.

We need to ask, "How do you know there is nothing outside the matter-space-time-energy continuum? How do you know that the instruments of physical measurement are the only ones that matter? How do you know there isn't something you can't measure with physical measuring tools? If all you have is a ruler, could you deny that weight exists?"

At the heart of the debate over stem cell research is the question of the personhood of a human embryo. If you hear someone insist that it's not life until implantation, then ask, "How do you know it's not a person? Isn't it genetically identical to the embryo ten minutes before implantation?"

Postmodern thought says that no one can know truth. This philosophy has permeated just about every college campus. To the professor who asserts, "No one can know truth," a student should ask, "How do you know that's true?" If that sounds slightly crazy to you, good! The professor does not know it's true, he or she only believes it to be true!

I often get hostile emails calling me stupid and biased for believing the Bible. I shouldn't put my faith, they say, in a book written by men and then mistranslated and changed over the centuries. Then I ask, "How do you know this is true?" I don't get answers back.

Shifting the burden of proof is quite legitimate. People are often just repeating what they have heard from others. But the other person can easily turn this weapon on you. We have to be ready to offer a defense for what we believe as well.

When you point to the Bible as your source of information, prepare to answer the killer question, "How do you know that's true?" You can, for example, point to fulfilled prophecy as evidence for the Bible's supernatural origin. Go to the "Reasons to Believe" section of Probe.org for a number of articles on why we can trust that the Bible is really God's word unchanged from the original manuscripts.

Many mistaken or deceived people believe in reincarnation and insist they remember their past lives. Shirley MacLaine claims to have been a Japanese geisha, a resident in Atlantis who commits suicide, an orphan raised by elephants, and the seducer of Charlemagne. Here's where this killer question comes in. "How do you know those are real memories and not just weird dreams? Did you remember them when you were a baby?"

So many people have embraced the pragmatic, expedient standard of, "Hey, it works for me."

- "It works for me to cheat on my taxes, as long as I don't get caught."

- "It works for me to spend hours on porn sites late at night since my wife doesn't know how to check the computer's history."

- "It works for me to keep God in his corner of the universe while I do my own thing; I'll get religious later in life."

To statements like this you should ask, "How do you know it works?" You haven't seen the whole, big picture. You can't know the consequences of today's choices.

Let me add a caveat here. Nobody likes to have his beliefs challenged. People may respond to "How do you know that's true?" in any variety of ways, but the implied counter-question is really, "Why should I believe you?" Be sure to ask with a friendly face and without an edge of superiority, sarcasm, or contempt.

Question #4: What if you're wrong?

One benefit of this question is that it keeps us focused on important stuff. On many issues, being wrong just doesn't matter a whole lot. If you're agonizing over a restaurant menu, trying to figure out the best entree, what if you're wrong? It doesn't matter. You can probably come back another time. But if you can't, will it wreck your life? Absolutely not.

Many of our youth (and adults as well) believe that having sex is just part of being social. For them, sex qualifies as recreation, much like an amusement park. Challenge this view: "What if you're wrong?" Aside from the high probability of sexually transmitted diseases, "casual" sex isn't, because of its lasting impact on the heart.

The ultimate question where this matters is, "What do you believe about God?" What do you do with Jesus' statement, "I am the way, the truth, and the life; no one comes to the Father except by Me"?

Suppose you believe there is no God, or that you can live however you want and God will let you into heaven because you're not a mass murderer. What if you're wrong? You will be separated from God forever!

It's only fair for us as followers of the Messiah to ask that of ourselves. What if we're wrong? What if we're actually living an illusion that there is a God and a purpose to life? I would say, "You know what? I still lived a great life, full of peace and purpose and fulfillment. Ultimately, if there were no God, it wouldn't matter—nothing would matter at all!—but I still loved my life. Either way, I win."

These four killer questions are powerful to spark meaningful conversation and encourage you and others to think critically. Use them wisely, be prepared for some interesting conversations . . . and have fun!

With the use of these four questions and the Bible as our spiritual arrows, we are now prepared to enter the five battlegrounds of the atheist. The next chapter lays down the challenges you will encounter.

THE CHALLENGE

(AQ) Questions you ask the Atheist to make him think)

To understand this book, you must know two concepts: atheism and agnosticism. According to Merriam-Webster, *"atheism"* means:

a) A lack of belief or a strong disbelief in the existence of a god or any gods.

b) A philosophical or religious position characterized by disbelief in the existence of a god or any gods.

Because atheism represents a general belief or philosophy, we do not capitalize it. It is not a formal religion with a founder and sacred texts. However, according to the *Routledge Encyclopedia of Philosophy*:

> *"Atheism is the position that affirms the non-existence of God. It proposes positive disbelief rather than mere suspension of belief."*

Atheists, under this definition, DO follow a religion. They create a false contradiction between God and reality. They claim that science must be naturalistic and secular. *Is this claim true?*

There are two types of science-historical and operational. Evolutionists and believers agree on operational science. This operational science will enable both observers the ability to observe, test and evaluate the results. The problem is historical science. Both will disagree with the other's version of historical science. It is this historical science that moves into the realm of religion.

WHAT IS AGNOSTICISM?

Agnosticism is the view that you cannot possibly know or prove the existence of God. Again, it is not a formal organized religion, so it is not capitalized.

Atheists reject God's existence, but agnostics are unwilling to decide either for or against it. They feel it is impossible to know either way. Their position is the ultimate fence straddle.

IS DOUBT REASONABLE?

Not atheist or agnostic? Congratulations, you believe in God. You are a *theist*. But the mere fact that people hold these other viewpoints may have you wondering—can you really know that God exists?

First, we should be wary of avoiding the evidence which clearly points to the existence of The Creator God.

Romans 1:18-19: *"God's anger is revealed from heaven against all the sin and evil of the people whose evil ways prevent the truth from being known. God punishes them, because what can be known about God is plain to them, for God Himself made it plain."*

Seekers who want 100% proof that God exists will be disappointed. The key to belief is not absolute certainty. Think of it more as sitting on a jury. The judge will instruct you that the defendant must be guilty "beyond a reasonable doubt." You need not be 100% certain of the defendant's guilt. You can have lingering doubts. But they should not be *reasonable* doubts.

A person who crosses a bridge can never be 100% certain they will make it safely to the other side. But that will not keep them from going across. They will cross with 95% certainty and 5% faith, but they must still go 100% across to the other side.

You must be careful of demanding so much evidence that you become immune to the evidence already before you. For some people, the amount of evidence will ever be enough.

In Luke 16:31, Jesus said in His parable: *"But Abraham said, 'If they will not listen to Moses and the prophets, they will not be convinced even if someone were to rise from death.'"*

It is normal to have doubts. We do not understand large parts of the universe. Often, people doubt God's existence because they do not understand or agree with what He does or allows. However, as finite human beings we should not expect to comprehend an infinite God.

THE SEVEN DIMENSIONS OF RELIGION

How do you know if your worldview is a religion?

With no deity, temples, or worship services, atheism may not seem like a religion, but don't be too quick to judge. First look for certain characteristics that religions have in common. Anthropologists and researchers use a framework called the "Seven Dimensions of Religion." It broadly covers the various aspects of religion without focusing on anything unique to a specific religion.

The dimensions are *narrative, experimental, social, ethical, doctrinal, ritual* and *material*. Not every religion has every dimension, nor are they all equally important for every religion. Let's look at these individually:

Narrative

Every religion has its stories. Almost all religions have stories explaining where the universe came from and humanity's part in it. The story, or narrative, is a very important feature of western atheism. *Why?*

A popular narrative for many atheists is evolution. Evolution is an explanation of where everything came from: the cosmos seemingly came out of nothing in a "big bang." Humans evolved from non-human creatures. Therefore, humanity's place in the cosmos is just another animal species of animal.

The believer's narrative comes from the stories in scripture. The first two chapters of Genesis lay the foundation and order of creation with humankind as the crown of it all. This lays the foundation for three major faiths: Judaism, Christianity, and Islam. These stories are incompatible with evolution.

Can you believe in both God and evolution? Some people try to, but anyplace they find the ideas in conflict, God loses. So who's really in control of that universe?

Experiential

This dimension refers to a shared experience among those who follow a religion. Many people feel certain emotions when they participate in certain religious ceremonies.

Believers channel their emotions and experiences through the word of God. It forms the basis of serving and helping others over self-gratification.

Atheists often believe they have freedom from religion. The denial of the divine involves the denial of an afterlife. Because of this, for the atheist, life has no higher purpose than happiness. Belief in evolution causes atheists to target free thinking and self-preservation. Some former atheists have reported a feeling of great release after converting.

Faith is also part of this dimension. Its meaning often gets twisted. To a believer, faith is trusting that God will fulfill his promises just as he has in the past.

Atheists may lack faith because they feel it means believing the impossible. Using that same definition, though, one would need incredible "faith" to believe that life could arise from non-life in violation of the laws of chemistry, physics, and biology.

Social

This dimension looks at the chain of command and power structures within the religion. In missionary religions, it also includes how new believers convert and how missionaries go about their work.

Prominent atheists will write books hoping to convert religious people to their worldview. This is exactly what a missionary of any religion hopes to do. This book aims to convert atheists to the believer's worldview.

Atheism doesn't have churches or Sunday school to teach its followers about its history and beliefs. However, it does have a form of institutionalized instruction in schools whose science classes cover evolution.

Doctrinal

Doctrines are the beliefs and philosophies that develop out of a religion. They originate from the stories. For Christians, the Trinity is an example. The Bible does not directly describe it, yet the concept logically flows from the Gospel account.

While atheism existed before Darwin, the idea of evolution provided an underpinning for new atheist doctrines. In 1933, it gave rise to secular humanism. The Humanist Manifestos of 1933, 1973, and 2003 outline the movement's doctrines, ethics and goals, and all accept evolution as true. Prominent atheists often use this as bible and source.

Ethical

From the stories and doctrines of a religion typically flow its ethics or morals—the rules and values by which you decide what is right and how to behave.

Atheists do not want to admit it, but atheism is a morally deficient religion. Most atheists adhere to one ethical system or another, but atheism ultimately has no foundation for morality. Some have created their own ethical systems, often based on the evolutionary the principle of "survival of the fittest." A related idea is *relativism,* the notion that you can do whatever you want if you can justify your actions based on the situation.

The believer's ethics come from the Bible. The Tenth Commandment, *"Do not covet,"* is an ethical commandment. When you believe your ethics come from God, they become *"absolute"* to you. They will justify themselves through scripture.

Ritual

In some religions, rituals have meanings attached to them. One such ritual is Passover commemorating the Israelites' escape from Egypt.

When you have no God to worship, rituals may seem pointless. However, many atheists do practice secular rituals such as birthdays and holidays, even those celebrated by other religions, such as Christmas and Easter. This is usually simply to maintain the tradition of a public holiday while rejecting its original meaning. In recent years, some atheists have begun public celebration of Darwin's birthday. (By sheer coincidence, he was born the exact same day as Abraham Lincoln.)

Material

The most important **dimension** of life quality is that which refers to **material** aspects. **Material dimension** represents all the economic conditions of people's **material** existence, as well as the satisfied needs, absolutely and relatively balanced in relation to human aspirations.

The believer's material dimension comes from the scriptures. It is verified by history, religious buildings and art, and the study of fossils and archeological sites.

The atheist's two extremes on the material dimension are as follows:

- Natural resources exist for exploitation because "survival of the fittest," gives humans, the fittest species, that right (a natural offshoot of the atheist's ethical views); or

- We should respect all of nature, particularly living things. To kill them is tantamount to murdering a cousin. This second view holds that all life is sacred.

Both of these ideas find support in evolution, but the second tends to be more common than the first. Here is the problem. Evolution cannot back up a single moral issue. The relationship and competition of all living creatures can justify being insanely cruel or insanely sentimental.

Conclusion

Prominent atheists often claim that their belief is not a religion. This allows them to evangelize in settings where other religions are illegal. Western atheism categorically has six of the seven dimensions of religion, and the remaining one, ritual, has also started to develop. Whatever the law might say, we can classify atheism as a religion.

(AQ) *By applying the seven dimensions of religion, how can you classify atheism as not being a religion?*

THE TWO GROUND RULES OF THEOLOGY

History can determine doctrine. In theology, if the doctrine would have been understood in the time period that the book was written, it can withstand the "stress" test. This process produces two ground rules of theology:

1. If the doctrine is new, it is not true.

2. If the doctrine is true, it cannot be new.

By abusing these rules, atheists can invade other people's faith. I have done it.

An atheist or agnostic will take the scriptures written centuries ago and try to place them into today's time frame. This is an unfair application of the rules.

As a believer, you must draw your atheist friend into the time when the scripture verse was written. Then you can both read it in context.

Context covers the history and customs of the time frame, both before and after the scripture appeared. Often the original language provides hidden meaning that tells whether and how you can apply the scripture today. Then you can disarm any negative feedback.

THE FIVE BATTLEFIELDS

If you are a believer hoping to convert an atheist, you must know their thinking process. You are most likely to encounter resistance, even counterattack, in one of these five major attack areas:

1) *Does God Exist?*
2) *Is the Bible True?*
3) *Is there a Resurrection?*
4) *Is Jesus God?*
5) *Is there another path to God?*

Number 2 is really the key to all of them, but if you can't prove the Bible, the atheist wins. If you have to answer the questions, the atheist is forcing you into their battlefield. Know this: You do not have to prove the atheist wrong. Reverse the battlefield. Make him demonstrate he is correct.

How do you do this? You do it with questions.

Consider the eagle versus the snake. The eagle does not fight the snake on the ground, where it is powerful and deadly. It picks up the snake and changes the battleground — or rather, the battle-sky. The snake has no stamina, no power, and no balance in the air.

Take your fight into the spiritual realm by praying. Then God takes over your battles. Don't fight the atheist in his comfort zone. Change the battlegrounds like the eagle and let God take charge through your earnest prayer. He will give you the questions you need.

(AQ) *Are you a 'Seeker of the Truth?' OR are you a closed-minded skeptic?*

An honest seeker is *someone willing to take an objective look at the evidence and make a decision*. Many people say they are honest seekers, but they never discover the truth about God. *Why?* They never look for it, and God never forces Himself upon people. He never compels non-seekers against their will.

THE ATHEIST'S PROBLEMS

We all have presumptions and prejudices that affect the way we view evidence. The atheist or agnostic typically has one or more of four major obstacles when seeking God:

1) Moralistic bias.

2) Inaccurate evidence (which leads to false convictions).

3) Mistaking tolerance for open-mindedness.

4) Faith. (Yes, an atheist must have faith!)

Let's look at these individually.

Moralistic Bias

An atheist can deny it, but the number one reason people reject Jesus is for *"the passion of sin."* Sin means rebellion against God. If God does not exist, sin has no meaning, and therefore you can do whatever you want without consequence.

An atheist/agnostic may decide to quit searching for God once they uncover evidence. They find that becoming a believer is not an *intellectual* issue. It is a *willingness* issue. If you accept that sin is real, then your morality will have to change.

Inaccurate Evidence

Many skeptics do not study the right evidence, causing them to make up their minds about God based upon hearsay information.

Hearsay is indirect information. Think of it as an overheard conversation (what you *hear* them *say*). Because of its unreliability, it is not admissible in a court of law. You should not use it in establishing a judgment about the existence of God.

Also consider this point: Most people do not reject Jesus. They are rejecting a false image of Jesus created by scriptures taken out of context. What if we apply this same process to evolution? Most skeptics become believers when they truly examine the evidence.

There are seven basic assumptions that are needed to justify the theory of evolution. Many evolutionists ignore the first six assumptions and consider the seventh.

1. Non-living matter produced living material. This is called "spontaneous generation."
2. Spontaneous generation only occurred once.
3. Viruses, bacteria, plants and animals are all interrelated
4. Protozoa became metazoa.
5. Various invertebrate phyla are interrelated.
6. Various invertebrate became the vertebrates.
7. Fish became amphibians, the amphibians became reptiles, and reptiles became birds and mammals.

The theory of evolution hold that all seven assumptions are valid, and these assumptions form the general theory of evolution. Here is the problem: the seven assumptions, by their nature, are not capable of experimental verification.

(AQ) *How do you apply ALL the seven assumptions to explain evolution?*

Again, I ask the question: *Are you a seeker of the truth or a closed-minded skeptic?*

Tolerance Mistaken for Open-mindedness

Today, one of the greatest virtues is tolerance. It has another word: relativism. That means, in today's language, "what is true for you may not be true for me." This process has moved people to assert that all religions are equally valid. Here is the problem: *How can all religions be valid when they all, at some points, contradict each other?*

Because of this contradiction, to believe in Jesus is momentous because He claims to have unique ownership of the truth. He does not say He's one of many truths but THE truth.

If you are truly an open-minded person, you must take this claim seriously. You must determine if any evidence which validates it — and if so, it is indeed the truth. (We will cover this in detail in the chapter: "Is Jesus the only way to God?")

Faith

(AQ) Again I ask: *"Are you a 'seeker of the truth or a closed-minded skeptic?"*

An atheist and believer both have faith. Only their belief systems differ. An atheist or agnostic needs to connect to the most basic level of faith, which most of us call "common sense." This is the initial requirement to becoming a believer in any belief system.

(AQ) *As an atheist, can you apply "common sense" to clarify your position in evolution? What happens when your belief system is challenged?*

If you close your mind to the challenge, is it because you are afraid of the results?

To trust in Jesus does not demand unrealistic faith. True faith rests on a solid foundation of evidence, embedded in trust. Faith produces assurance. Delaying a faith decision is spiritually dangerous because indecision can become a permanent position.

Remember this: Where faith is required, doubt is possible. God's requirement of faith also allows the rejection of God. Despite the possibility of doubt, honest seekers can truly find God.

(AQ) *Are you an honest seeker? Are you willing to follow the evidence wherever it will lead you?*

If you're a truly honest seeker, you cannot be an atheist. You must at least be an agnostic. This book will help remove an agnostic from straddling between belief and doubt. After following the logic of this book, you will find it hard to prove that God does not exist.

If you are a believer and know an atheist or an agnostic, this book gives to give you a path for discussion to change their position.

With this introduction, let's start with the first battlefield, *"Does God Exist?"*

DOES GOD EXIST?

(AQ) Questions you ask the Atheist to make him think)

GOD EXISTS-THE EVIDENCE.

(AQ) *If you were on a jury, how much evidence would you require to convict or acquit? Would you convict on circumstantial evidence only or would you want as much evidence as you can get? Would you want from only one source or many sources?*

The Bible is not the only source of knowledge that gives evidence of the existence of God. Consider the following evidences:

- Evidence from Physics
- Evidence from Biology
- Evidence from Biochemistry
- Evidence from Genetics
- Evidence from Mathematics
- Evidence from Paleontology
- Evidence from Anthropology
- Evidence from Astronomy
- Evidence from Cosmology
- Evidence from Revelation

THE FLAWS OF EVOLUTION

In 1859, Charles Darwin published *On the Origin of Species*. His theory of evolution centered on the concept of "survival of the fittest." The fittest organisms pass their survival attributes to their offspring in the form of superior genes. This theory makes the assertion that modern animals came into existence through natural processes.

Darwin's 1871 follow-up, *The Descent of Man*, advanced his theory that man and ape were descendants of a common ancestor.

This flouted the general belief that God created the universe and man. Atheists latched onto Darwin's ideas as scientific proof of God's nonexistence.

In 1922, a Tennessee high school teacher stood trial for unlawfully teaching evolution in what history would remember as the "Scopes Monkey Trial." Though he lost the case, the national media painted John Scopes as an intelligent man fighting an outdated law written by backward country hicks.

Soon evolution become a universally accepted fact. Creation, and by extension belief in God, became associated with pre-scientific myths. Many gave up their belief in God to maintain their newly found faith and belief in evolution.

Consider this: The theory of evolution can produce the loss of faith in God because it runs counter to the supernatural creation of the Bible. The theory of evolution has remained unproven for over 150 years.

There are several flaws in the theory of evolution.

In Darwin's own texts, he never gave one single example of any new species of plants or animals coming from natural selection. No scientist has witnessed evolution taking place in the past, nor can anyone see it happening today.

You can find many examples of microevolution (changes within species), but none for macroevolution (one species bringing forth another). We have no documented example of any organism evolving into a new, more complex species (the "molecules to man" theory). Past evidence shows that extinction and not evolution has prevailed.

Evolution cannot account for the origin of life. It seems to require that life arose from nonliving matter. How could this happen?

Suppose scientists in a lab managed to produce life. Would that prove that non-life could create life? **No!** Rather, it would prove the opposite. It would show that only with great effort could an intelligent being (or beings) reproduce what is already in existence. This would show that life takes **intelligence** to create.

Evolutionists theorized that what intelligent humanity cannot accomplish somehow happened by chance under conditions that no longer exist. What does that mean? The evolutionist has to resort to a hypothetical atmosphere, a hypothetical ocean composition, and a hypothetical process. And the primitive organisms thereby created are hypothetical as well, because they also no longer exist. That is not scientific at all!

(AQ) *Where is your physical evidence that is accepted through a court of law that life started from non-life?*

THE DISCOVERY OF DNA

Modern research has shown that natural selection is not capable of creating anything new. Darwin was unaware of the DNA and chromosomes within each living organism. It proves that natural selection does not produce new genes. It only selects among pre-existing characteristics.

Natural selection cannot create new traits without some kind of genetic mutation. No one has ever observed a beneficial mutation. All have resulted in deterioration. Evolutionists have speculated that somewhere in the past, beneficial mutations occurred. If they did, they would only change the organism's existing characteristics. That cells would have had to mutate to create a fully functioning eye is unthinkable.

Today, scientists continue to promote evolution as a fact. However, this is not because of the evidence. The notion of a divine creation is not viable in the minds of many people. It seems like superstition. This is not science but philosophy. Evolution has a prejudice against the supernatural, so it twists scientific facts to exclude a Creator.

To believe in the theory of evolution requires a great deal of faith in many illogical and impossible scenarios.

Far more evidence supports the theory of Creation. Belief in God, the Creator, is not superstition.. Faith in God rests upon solid, scientific and historical evidence.

Most non-believers reject God not because they have examined the evidence, but because of their own preconceived ideas. They never had, nor wanted to have, the intellectual integrity to examine the evidence.

(AQ) *Again, I ask you "Are you an honest seeker? Are you willing to follow the evidence wherever it will lead you?"*

EVIDENCE FROM PHYSICS

The laws of thermodynamics are the greatest blow to evolution. They are accepted by all reputable scientists.

A) The First Law of Thermodynamics.

This is the law of energy conservation. It means that the amount of mass and energy is constant. Mass and energy are interchangeable, but neither can be created nor destroyed. Because the energy existing today cannot be re-created, it is impossible for the present universe to have created itself. What does this mean? Because natural processes cannot create energy, energy had to come from an "outside agency," a source external to this present universe.

(AQ) *When has anyone ever proven this First Law of Thermodynamics wrong?*

B) The Second Law of Thermodynamics.

This is the law of entropy. It states that all the available energy in the universe is decreasing. It will eventually die of heat-death as all the molecules in the universe continue to move in increasingly random patterns. They can never become organized again.

Isaiah 51:6: *"Look up to the heavens! Look around you at the earth below! The skies will disappear like clouds of smoke. The earth will become like worthless old clothes. The people on earth will die, but my salvation will continue forever. My goodness will never end."*

Our universe is running out of usable fuel. The moment a star is born, it uses up massive amounts of hydrogen.

Because of its limited supply, the universe cannot be eternal. *What does this mean?* Because the universe is dying, tine cannot be infinite. If you pushed the start of the universe back far enough, it would have already fizzled out. Therefore the universe **had** to have a beginning.

Evolution requires billions of years and multiple violations of the Second Law to have occurred, making it statistically impossible. When you truly understand the Laws of Thermodynamics, they refute the theory of evolution. *Why?* It is because the created universe could not have created itself, it **must** have a Creator.

(AQ) *How would you use this Second Law of Thermodynamics through evolution?*

EVIDENCE FROM BIOLOGY

The universe is perfectly designed for supporting intelligent life forms. The earth has a great number of complex organisms that defy any naturalistic explanation. It contains over 11 million different species, each representing an amazing design of engineering and life.

Every intelligent design shows is the existence of a Designer. The greater the design, the greater the Designer. The complex structure of the universe declares that it had to have a great Architect. When we speak of "Mother Nature," we refer to the great intelligence behind nature.

Consider the following biological evidence:

Example: The Human Brain

The brain weighs about three pounds, yet it can do things no massive supercomputer can.

It has up to 15 billion neurons, each one a living unit within itself. It has over 100 trillion (10 to the 14th power) electrical connections. This is more than all the electrical connections in all the electrical appliances in the world. Every cubic inch of the brain contains a minimum of 100 million nerve cells interconnected by 10 thousand miles of fibers to other nerve cells in the brain.

Because of this vast number of unique connections, to assemble an object resembling the human brain would take an eternity even when applying the most sophisticated engineering techniques.

(AQ) *Could this Design and Engineering have occurred by accident? Where is your evidence?*

Now add this to the complexity: a man's brain is completely different from a woman's.

At conception, the male sperm determines the child's sex. The woman's egg will always have an X chromosome. If the sperm also has an X chromosome, the child will be a girl. If the sperm has a Y chromosome, the child will be male.

You can change your exterior in myriad ways, from weightlifting to tattoos to so-called "gender reassignment surgery." Regardless, your brain will always be the brain prepared for you at the beginning of your formation.

(AQ) *Could this Design and Engineering have occurred by accident? Where is your evidence?*

Example: The Human Eye

The human eye contains 130 million light-sensitive rods and cones which generate photo-chemical reactions that convert light into electrical impulses. One billion impulses travel to the brain every second. The eye can make over 100 thousand separate motions. When confronted with darkness, it can increase its light intake 100,000 times. It comes complete with precision aiming and focusing and automatic maintenance during sleep.

Here is the problem for evolution to work: Thousands of chance mutations must accidentally be formed–but this is impossible. Also, within the evolutionary framework, just the eye itself still would need to evolve several times in different species like squids and houseflies. The human eye is so sophisticated that scientists still do not fully understand it. This, too, points to an intelligent Designer.

(AQ) *If it does not point to an intelligent designer, can you explain how evolution can produce an eye?*

Example: The Cell

During Darwin's day the cell was thought to be a simple design. Today, we know it is highly complex.

A simple bacteria cell is only .001 millimeter wide, yet we might call it a sophisticated chemical factory in its complexity. A single self-contained bacteria cell has thousands of functions and tasks: energy generators, defensive systems, transport systems, food factories, protection barriers, waste removal structures and communication processes.

Consider this: Human beings have up to 100 billion of these self-contained cellular cities, and each of the cells all work together to carry out the functions of life.

(AQ) *How does evolution explain these complex structures that exist within each cell? Please explain the process if not by an intelligent designer.*

EVIDENCE FROM BIOCHEMISTRY

Biochemistry is the chemistry of living systems. This field is important to the study of the origin of life and gives our discussion two important foundations: Biogenesis and Teleonomy.

Biogenesis

In 1938, the theory of *abiogenesis* postulated that the first forms of life came from *"a primordial soup of complex chemicals through reactions with electrical discharges under an assumed reducing (no-oxygen) primordial atmosphere."* In short, life originated from chance by complex chemicals.

Again, here is the problem: The inorganic cannot give rise to the organic. Biogenesis is just a sophisticated repackaging of *spontaneous generation*, the long-debunked idea of life coming from non-life matter.

Louis Pasteur destroyed the idea of "spontaneous generation of life" in 1862 by demonstrating that bacteria, and other forms of life, could not develop from sterile material. Biogenesis forces evolutionists into two non-scientific assumptions:

- Spontaneous generation actually occurred for some unknown reason in some hypothetical primordial sea, AND

- It occurred only once.

Biogenesis requires creation.

(AQ) *How did life originate? If you accept these non-scientific assumptions, what is the complex process that creates life from non-life? Where is your evidence?*

Evolution requires that spontaneous generation must have occurred. Know this: **Not one single case of spontaneous generation has ever been observed.** All scientific observations point to *biogenesis*, the fact that **life comes from life**. If you want to get life, you need life.

(AQ) *If you disagree with this, can you explain how life can start from non-life? Where is your evidence?*

Teleonomy

Chemistry has verified a fundamental difference between living and nonliving things. The difference found in the living things is teleonomy.

To understand teleonomy, compare a dead stick to a living tree. The living tree uses nutrients and energy from the sun to grow. But the same solar energy on the dead stick only serves to speed up its decay process.

For a spontaneous generation to occur, the forces of chemicals and energy together would only have worked if the tree DNA already existed. Without this pre-existing design, the living tree would not have existed. Here is the point: **it takes intelligence to create!**

(AQ) *Again, if you disagree with this, how do you explain life from non-life without destroying the first and second laws of thermodynamics?*

EVIDENCE FROM GENETICS

As mentioned before, all forms of life are dependent upon **DNA** (Deoxyribonucleic Acid) molecules. DNA programs the characteristics of each organism. It determines a human's height, hair color, and arrangement of 206 bones, 600 muscles, 10,000 auditory nerve fibers, 2 million optic nerve fibers, 100 billion nerve cells, and 400 billion feet of blood vessels and capillaries. All of this material that contains the physical processes of life is intelligently **coded**.

DNA functions like a computer program. A program is a series of steps taken to accomplish a goal. No natural source can produce this code. It must come from intelligence.

Example: The ameba's DNA has enough storage for information to contain the information in a thousand-book set of encyclopedias. If you stretched out the 46 segments of DNA in a human cell, it would be about seven feet long.

(AQ) *How did this DNA originate? Could this coded, complex program have started by accident? If it did, which came* *first – DNA without the cell, or the cell without the DNA? How would you back your answer?*

EVIDENCE FROM MATHEMATICS
God's Existence through Mathematics

Evolutionists argue that with enough time, even the most improbable events become probable. They say that life for evolve by chance would require billions of years. However, evolution is still impossible even according to their principles of probability.

Consider this: according to the book *When Skeptics Ask*, page 22, *"the odds of a one celled animal emerging by evolution by chance is one in 10 to the 40,000th power."* From the book *Communication with Extraterrestrial Intelligence*, pages 45–46, *"the chances of man evolving is one in 10 to the 2,000,000,000th power."*

Let's put these odds in perspective. When you consider that 5 billion years is only 10 to the 17th seconds and the visible universe contains less than 10 to the 80th atoms, the odds are not only staggering, they are impossible.

Borel's *"Single Law of Chance"* states that the odds of one in 10 to the 50th power is *"impossible."* This equates with the odds of a tornado blowing through a junkyard containing all the loose parts of a 747 jet, accidentally assembling the parts correctly, and making it ready for flight. The universe occurring by mere chance is not a scientific option.

What does *"by chance"* mean? Webster defines *chance* as *"something that happens because of unknown or unconsidered forces."* To understand this, let's consider the act of flipping of a coin. *What makes a coin come up heads or tails?*

The coin starts out facing one way or the other. The flipper has a certain amount of thumb strength and technique. A certain amount of speed and pressure rotates the coin. Combine this with the density of the air and it will produce a specific number of revolutions.

Once we know all these facts, we know *exactly* why a coin lands as heads or tails. Therefore, based on the definition, chance was not **the cause**. Rather, chance is a non-entity with no power to **cause** anything.

An example of a chance is the rolling of a dice. The result will be 1. 2. 3. 4. 5. Or 6. The outcome has an equal chance of happening.

Therefore, if the chances of evolution are as high as one in 10 to the 1000th, then what are the chances that the universe happened by a *known* force—i.e., creation? That would be far greater than 99.9%, making creation infinitely more probable. If these are the only possibilities available, then you can conclude that creation must have occurred.

(AQ) *If the "Single Law of Chance" says the odds of 10 to the 50th power is impossible, and the chances of evolution is 1 in 10 to the 1000th, how do you lower the odds to allow evolution to exist?*

CREATION OF MAN AND THE HEBREW LETTERS

The human body's design shows a surprising connection to the Hebrew alphabet and numbers significant to God. The human skull has 22 cranial and facial bones, which is also the number of the letters in the Hebrew alphabet.

The upper part of the skull consists of eight bones: frontal (forehead), occipital, ethmoid, sphenoid, left and right parietal, and left and right temporal. Eight represents the letter Chet, whose picture is the ladder. (Borrowed into the Latin alphabet, it became our eighth letter, H.) It represents transcendence, the power to reach a higher level.

The neck contains seven cervical vertebrae, which support the skull and organs of the neck. The first, called the atlas, supports and balances the head. The second allows the head to move to the right or left. The other five bones connect the skull to the spine. Seven represents the Hebrew letter Zayin, which means completion and a symbol of authority. (Much more about seven is coming up.)

Humans have twelve ribs, T1 to T12. This connects to the twelve tribes of Israel. The male T12 rib bone is a *floating rib*. It does not connect to the ribcage. The woman's T12 does. I believe that it is this rib that God used to create Eve.

Humans have ten fingers and ten toes. The number ten represents the Hebrew letter Yod. It is the divine point of energy. Since the Yod forms all of the other letters, and since God uses the letters as the building blocks of creation, Yod indicates in Hebrew God's omnipresence.

One more point: there are five lumbar vertebrae, L1 through L5. The fifth Hebrew letter is the letter Hay. This letter also represents the name of God.

(AQ) *If the body was formed by evolution, what would be the purpose for the man only to have a 'floating rib? What are the odds of evolution producing these possibilities?*

The Number Seven

What do the Sabbath, Joshua's march around Jericho and the pairs of clean animals brought by Noah into the ark all have in common? The answer is that at their heart all these biblical subjects have the number **seven**. The Bible is full of sevens. It's not just in these stories. In the Gospel of John, Jesus speaks of himself using the phrase "*I am*" seven times. What is so special about seven?

In ancient Israel, the number seven represented divine perfection. It was considered a powerful, unbreakable number because it could not be divided by common small numbers which people used to count on a single hand.

The word for seven in Hebrew—*sheva* is linked to *shevu*—an oath. When someone wanted to make a very strong promise, they would take an oath as though to say: "let the divinely perfect number seven be my witness that I..."

Seven was the most sacred number to the Hebrews: *"By the SEVENTH day God completed His work"* (Genesis 2.2). The "Feast of Booths" was complete after SEVEN days (Leviticus 23.34).

SEVEN pairs of each *"clean"* animal went onto the ark (Genesis 7.2). In Revelation we find SEVEN "churches" (in all forms). Judgment of the earth occurs via a SEVEN-sealed book, SEVEN trumpets and SEVEN bowls of wrath. Counting from Adam, we get approximately SIX millennia on the earth; the SEVENTH millennium will see the Messiah's rule on earth, and complete earth's history.

The number SEVEN is so important that it seems to place God's stamp on the living world around us, specifically in the physiology of living organisms.

Our seven-day week is not just because of the seven days of creation; it has genuine biological significance. God's mathematics in creation created a *circaseptan* ("about seven") rhythm, which is a built-in cycle of seven days around which many biological processes of life revolve.

The Week in History

Today, we take the seven-day cycle for granted. But in ancient cultures, "weeks" varied in length from three to nineteen days. But in the millennium before the Messiah, Israel's seven-day week took over the world. Their weekly cycle revolved around something unique.

Only the Jews—those careful keepers of God's time—made sure to preserve one day as a period of rest and reflection. This is a *"Sabbath"* during which to focus on spiritual matters.

As the centuries rolled on, the Jewish Sabbath became an accepted part of Roman society. The ancient historian Josephus, in his book *Against Apion*, said, *"The masses have long since shown a keen desire to adopt our religious observances; and there is not one city, Greek or barbarian, nor a single nation, to which our custom of abstaining from work on the seventh day has not spread."*

BIOLOGICAL RHYTHMS

It seems that all life moves in seven-day rhythms. A growing number of scientists have embraced an entirely new field of study known as chronobiology that examines repeating biological rhythms in living organisms. .

Franz Halberg of the University of Minnesota is widely considered the *"father of chronobiology."* He works in an office in Romania crammed with bookshelves stacked with copies of journals and papers he's produced over the years.

He insists that humans don't just experience circadian rhythms of approximately 24 hours, we also operate under *circaseptan* or weekly rhythms. Circaseptan rhythms also occur in simple plant life.

Halberg first became interested in the subject when, as a high school student, he accompanied physician friends of his parents in their practice. He began to notice that patients with pneumonia either recovered or died in seven days.

Today, he proposes that body rhythms of that length do not result passively from the social cycle of the calendar week. Instead they are innate, self-governing, and perhaps the reason the calendar week arose in the first place.

The human body has an approximate seven-day clock. The science of chronobiology describes circaseptan rhythms in the body that run about seven days in length. This is a very good reason to rest every seven days (Exodus 20:10)! The ten-day week of the humanistic French Revolution and the "continuous work week" of the Russian Revolution both failed for this very reason.

Researchers report "a built-in (genetically determined) about-seven-day (*circaseptan*) period" in connection with human organ transplants. Swelling or rejection of an organ transplant tends to occur about seven or fourteen (7 × 2) days after surgery. This rhythm also seems to apply to the immune response to infections, blood and urine chemicals, blood pressure, and the common cold.

A woman's fertility cycle has multiples of seven. In a short cycle of 21 days, ovulation occurs around day 7. The average fertility cycle is 28 days (7 × 4). In a long cycle of 35 days, ovulation does not occur until around day 21 (7 × 3). The adult human body contains around 7,000,000,000,000,000,000,000,000,000 (7 octillion) atoms

In obstetrics, the human gestation period is around 280 days (7 × 40). The gestation period for a dog is typically 63 days (7 × 9). The gestation period for a sheep is typically 147 days (7 × 21). The gestation period for a domestic duck is typically 28 days (7 × 4).

Rhythm of Life

Life on this earth seems to have calibrated in some mysterious way to the number seven. The moon also takes about seven days to reach each of its four phases.

The number seven even governs the music world. How many notes in an octave? Most people will say eight, just as there are eight sides to an octagon. But no, an octave has only seven. Count them: *do, re, me, fa, so, la, ti — and then* we start over again with *do*. That eighth note, the octave, begins a new cycle of seven. The musical scale has only seven unique notes; that's why we have no key of H (the eighth letter). This is "inclusive reckoning," where a complete cycle must include the start of the next one.

(AQ) *How did evolution create these different cycles based on the number seven? Where is your evidence?*

Six around One

A hexagon (six-sided object) provides the most efficient use of space. Just ask a bee busily building his honeycomb. Mathematicians and architects insist that a hexagonal room (six walls built around a floor — the *"six around one"* principle) provides the most efficient perimeter-to-area ratio and requires the least amount of wall material per square foot of floor space.

Like that central circle set in the middle of six workdays, the Sabbath is God's original prescription for allowing His people to enjoy optimum health, spirituality, and longevity. *"Six days you shall labor,"* He says in Exodus 34:21, *"but on the seventh day you shall rest; even during the plowing season and harvest you must rest."*

Seven-day Cycles

Research has uncovered many human conditions that seem to rise and fall in seven-day cycles. They include:

- heartbeat
- blood pressure
- body temperature
- hormone levels
- acid content in blood
- red blood cell count
- oral temperature
- female breast temperature
- urine chemistry and volume
- the ratio between norepinephrine and epinephrine, two important neurotransmitters
- the flow of several body chemicals such as the stress-coping hormone cortisol

Even the common cold has a *seven-day* cycle.

Doctors have long observed that response to malaria infection and pneumonia crisis peaks at seven days. Chicken pox symptoms (a high fever and small red spots) usually appear almost exactly two weeks after exposure to the illness. A person will tend to have an increase in swelling on the seventh and then the fourteenth day after surgery.

Organ transplants face similar crises as the body's immune system attacks the newly introduced foreign object.

(AQ) *How do you explain these 7-day processes by evolution? Where is your evidence?*

In the Blood

God knew all of this because He created us. Perhaps that's why He commanded, in Genesis 17:12, that male babies should undergo circumcision one week after birth. (Some scholars still don't realize that "on the eighth day" is the Hebrew way of saying "one week later" — the eighth day of the Jewish week was the first day of the next week Leviticus 23:39).

The Hebrews used inclusive reckoning when speaking of time, just as we do with the notes of the octave. In other words, God told the Israelites to circumcise their children on the octave of their day of birth.

Why wait a week? Because doctors tell us that's when the blood has its maximum level of prothrombin, which causes the blood to clot and prevent endless bleeding. It's never as high again.

Symphony Players

We live in a universe, not a multiverse. All of life is a symphony, and we're each players in God's great orchestra. Every song has a cadence, a rhythm. When we're "in the groove" with the conductor, our lives experience a certain serenity, a familiar flow. Once we get out of step with the cadence of the song — the rhythm of time — our lives falter.

Imagine if you tried to follow a 30-hour day. You'd soon find yourself completely out of step with society. Human nature is locked into that natural, God-created 24-hour rhythm.

The same is true of the weekly seven-day rhythm. That means that if you're working on the Sabbath, you are breaking yourself.

Maybe that's one of the reasons why Seventh-Day Adventists — a denomination of Christian believers who observe the seventh-day Sabbath — tend to live seven to ten years longer than the average citizen. They're simply in sync with the rhythm of life.

Custom or Creation

One final question. *How do we know that these rhythms aren't just social or religious customs?* Perhaps, after several thousand years, the weekly cycle has simply become inbred by social convention.

The problem with this explanation is that it can't account for *seven-day* rhythms in algae, Dahl rats, mice, guinea pigs, honeybees, beach beetles, and face flies.

In his writings, author Jeremy Campbell reports that *seven-day* rhythms *"are of very ancient origin, appearing in primitive one-celled organisms, and are thought to be present even in bacteria, the simplest form of life now existing."*

Here's something really intriguing: while human teeth are growing, small lines or ridges form on the dental enamel about every seven days. We might say the growing tooth exhibits a weekly *"rest"* as it leaves behind a dark marker (just as trees show darker rings where their growth pauses in the winter).

Before we continue, consider this definition: The word *"hominid"* means *"a primate of a family that includes humans and their fossil ancestors."* This understanding will be helpful.

According to scientific researchers A. Mann, J. Monge, and M. Lampl in their book *Investigation Into the Relationship Between Perikymata Counts and Crown Formation Times*, these lines — 30-40 microns apart — are called *striae of Retzius*. These slight ridges or groves appear even on the teeth of fossil hominids that lived before modern culture existed.

Why Seven?

Why should all living things have an innate seven-day cycle? I'd like to suggest a not-too-wild theory. *"In six days the Lord made the heavens and the earth, the sea, and all that is in them, but he rested on the seventh day. Therefore the Lord blessed the Sabbath day and made it holy"* (Exodus 20:11).

God put within us rhythms that flow from the internal logic of our bodies. Isaiah 58 is a chapter containing some potent health secrets. The first is a promise that God will bless those who bless the less fortunate (verses 5-12). The second is that God will bless those who honor His holy day.

"If you keep your feet from breaking the Sabbath and from doing as you please on my holy day, if you call the Sabbath a delight and the Lord's holy day honorable, and if you honor it by not going your own way and not doing as you please or speaking idle words, then you will find your joy in the Lord, and I will cause you to ride on the heights of the land" (verses 13, 14).

Just as we tune our radios to receive our favorite musical broadcasts, so every living cell has embedded in its primal genetic material a resonant frequency — a clock, a beat that puts us in sync with the universe. That powerful, mysterious beat revolves around the number seven.

(AQ) *How would you explain the seven-day cycle in all living things without a Designer / Creator? Where is your evidence?*

EVIDENCE FROM PALEONTOLOGY

Paleontology is the study of the fossils. The fossil records have often been cited as one of the main evidences for evolution. In the general theory of evolution, the basic progression of life is:

- Non-living matter
- Protozoans
- Metazoan invertebrates
- Vertebrate fishes
- Amphibians
- Reptiles (with a branch leading to dinosaurs and then birds)
- Mammals
- Apes
- Man

If evolution were true, one would expect to find the transitional sequences from one species to another, but in the mile-deep fossil graveyard around the world, huge gaps exist in the fossil record.

(AQ) *Where are the millions of creatures that should be part–reptile and part–bird, or part-ape and part–human? Where is your evidence?*

Occasionally you will hear that someone has found an unusual fossil like a dinosaur with feathers or a fish with leg-like appendages. They will call it the long-sought *"missing link"* between the species. That term is deceiving. There should not be one intermediate link but rather, thousands of them.

The formation of fossils demands that the organisms undergo a quick burial in an environment free of oxygen where nothing will disturb them. We find few places like this on earth today. Flood conditions are ideal for forming fossils, and the global Flood described in Genesis provides a starting point to examine the fossil record.

Rather than the gradual changes of one organism transforming into another, the fossil record shows fully formed creatures appearing suddenly and then disappearing. This is just what we would expect if God created these various life forms and then later destroyed them by the Flood.

Some of the greatest testimonies to a worldwide flood are the many, massive fossil graveyards across the globe. One of the most popular in the United States is Dinosaur

National Monument near Vernal, Utah. *"The Wall"* (as it is called) is an exposed sandstone graveyard which contains the fossilized remains of dinosaurs, freshwater clams and snails, logs, and many other organisms.

It is believed the remains are a result from a dried-up waterhole where many dinosaurs perished 150 million years ago. After the drought, the river filled up again and slowly covered the carcasses with sand and gravel, and the fossilization process began. Could this explanation and process be true?

No. That is not how fossils form, let alone a layer called *"The Wall"* in Utah. Fossilization requires quick burial in an environment that lacks oxygen. Otherwise, scavengers and bacteria will quickly decompose the organisms. The most common fossils at the site are freshwater clams. When clams are open, they are dead. When they are closed, they are alive. Most of these clam shells are found opened, showing that they were buried after death.

However, some of the clams are found still closed, indicating that they were buried while still alive. That could not have happened if the river and waterhole had dried up.

That explanation from the Park Service also fails to mention the large amounts of volcanic sediments found at the site. That, combined with mud flows from the Flood, makes a much better explanation for this fossil graveyard and many others around the world.

Creation scientists believe the fossil record resulted from one Flood while evolutionists suggest it was many small catastrophes.

Consider this: One of the most common ways fossilization occurs is when the pores of a bone or piece of wood fill with mineral-rich water that forms crystals. Once a miner's hat fell into limey water and then hardened to stone, proving that fossilization can be rapid. As with oil and coal, laboratory processes can produce fossils in a very short time.

"Fossilized jellyfish found in Wisconsin" was a January 2002 headline in the Washington Post. These jellyfish must have fossilized very rapidly because any jellyfish that washed up on the shore today disintegrate in a matter of hours. They have no bone structure. The formation containing these outgrown fossils covers a large area and includes millions of specimens of other organisms. These all must have been buried in a short period, in wet, sandy conditions to preserve them.

Evolutionists teach that sedimentary rock takes millions of years to form, but we all know concrete can form solid rock in hours. Time, heat, and pressure can and do alter the properties of rock but are unnecessary to form it.

The presence of fossils from marine and terrestrial organisms in graveyards around the world cannot be explained by the slow processes. The Green River Formation, a fossil-rich field in Wyoming, includes birds, bats, fish, insects, and many plant species all buried together.

The Redwall Limestone of Grand Canyon contains fossil nautiloids (squid-like creatures with a shell) and other marine creatures buried by a fast-moving slurry (a watery mixture of insoluble matter, such as mud, lime, or plaster of Paris) that involved 24 cubic miles of lime, sand, and silt.

How can we account for the massive scale of these graveyards? Many geologists today are re-examining fossilization as the result of catastrophic events — though not necessarily the biblical catastrophe.

The large scale of Redwall, as well as other similarly featured locations around the world, are best explained by the global Flood as described in Genesis.

Contrary to popular belief, rocks and fossils actually form quite rapidly. The exquisitely preserved fish fossils we find across the globe would require quick burial in an environment that would prohibit decomposition. We do not encounter these conditions in very many lakes and rivers on earth today.

Rather than millions of years, rocks can change over observable time periods, similar to the everyday process of making concrete from a mixture of lime, sand, and gravel. The organisms trapped in rapidly deposited layers are the most likely to fossilize. The ideal way to make a fossil of your pet fish would be to add quickly some concrete mix to the bowl.

Extensive coal beds and oil reservoirs are also examples of fossil graveyards. The textbooks explain coal beds as the remains of plants gathered in shallow seas and swamps over geologic time periods. Pictures of lush landscapes with foreign plants and giant insects make the story more believable. One problem is that we do not see swamps forming coal today. Embedded fossils like compressed bark sheets and pine trees do not match the forest descriptions given by the textbooks.

The presence of carbon-14 in coal samples also suggests recent formation. The Flood can explain the rapid burial of enormous amounts of vegetation that became the coal we use today. We can generate coal, as well as oil and natural gas, within hours in the laboratory—not the alleged "millions of years."

Thousands of creatures living today are virtually identical to their ancestors which supposedly lived hundreds of millions of years ago. These include many insects, the Wollemi pine, ginkgo trees, crocodiles, coelacanths, and many marine invertebrates.

How can evolution explain that some creatures have remained unchanged for such long periods of time while others have changed rapidly? There is no real consistent answer.

Is it is due to long generation times? That doesn't work for cockroaches and bacteria that reproduce in days or minutes. Is it chance and luck? The atheist may accept it, but that choice is intellectually unsatisfying to many scientists.

Is it because of the lack of habitat change? That only works in a few examples.

(AQ) *Can you, as an evolutionist, clearly explain why these "living fossils" are still with us today? Where is your evidence?*

Creationists can. They understand that the ancestors of these organisms were created only six thousand years ago. So they have survived relatively unchanged for only a few thousand years, not millions.

Many rock layers that are thousands of feet above sea level contain fossils of marine organisms. Even the top of the

Himalayas has fossil marine organisms in the limestone. *How do we explain this?*

At some point, the ocean waters must have covered the continents. The continents could not have been lower because the less dense continental rock *"floats"* on the mantle well above the ocean rocks.

Two mechanisms can explain how the water covered the continents.

First, during the biblical Flood, the fountains of the great deep would have added water to the oceans for 150 days.

Second, if the ocean floor rose, it would have pushed the sea level up and caused the water to flood across the continents. This could result from light, molten rock breaking through the crust to create the newly forming seafloor.

Thus the Flood transported marine organisms onto the continents. Later, as the mountains rose and the new ocean floor rock cooled and sank, these sediments rose high above sea level, depositing fossils on the mountaintops. By looking to the Bible, we can explain the world in a consistent way.

Genesis 7:11 reads, *"On the 17th day of the second month, when Noah was 600 years old,* <u>the springs under the earth broke through the ground, and water flowed out</u>

everywhere. *The sky also opened like windows and rain poured down. The rain fell on the earth for 40 days and 40 nights. That same day Noah went into the boat with his wife, his sons Shem, Ham, and Japheth, and their wives."*

Evolutionists suggest that the fossils in the geologic record show a progression of life from the bottom to the top. They claim the "fact of evolution" is present in the rock record in the evolutionary story. Bottom–dwelling marine creatures fossilized first, and then other sea creatures followed by the strata of life on the land.

However, creation scientists view the rock record as a testimony to the global Flood as described in Genesis. The differing life-forms in the rock units represent different ecological zones buried in succession during the Flood.

(AQ) *Based on how fossils are formed, how can jellyfish, with no bone structure, fossilize?*

The geographical record does not reveal the gradual evolution of organisms but rather the sudden appearance of fully developed forms of life. The fossil records show that millions of plants and animals have lived and died on earth, destroyed not over many ages but a single age.

A century ago, evolutionists promised we would see the gaps in the fossil record filled, but they *still* remain. The study of fossilization has revealed billions and billions of fossils preserved *abnormally*. Again, we have uncovered massive graveyards that contain various animals from different climatic areas all buried together.

This points to a worldwide water cataclysm, which is consistent with the destruction described by the Genesis flood. This flood explains why fossils from one supposed evolutionary age have mixed in with fossils from another age.

Evidence in the fossil record is embarrassing to the theory of evolution. *Why?* It is because the fossil record show that creation has occurred.

(AQ) *If evolution exists, how do you explain why the fossils from one evolutionary age are being found mixed in with fossils from other ages? Where is your evidence?*

EVIDENCE FROM ANTHROPOLOGY.

Remember this definition? The word *"hominid"* means *"a primate of a family that includes humans and their fossil ancestors."* Evolutionists claim man evolved from apes by way of a pre-human form of life. They call this form of life "hominids."

There are many fossils of **true humans** and **true apes**, but *none* of the purported *"ape-human."* Evolutionists, eager to prove they are right, have often prematurely publicized evidence and later retracted it when proven wrong. The existence of the alleged "ape-human" ancestors does not come from any solid evidence, but rather the imagination of good artists.

The facts do not support the many failed attempts to find the *"ape-human."* It does, however, support the biblical evidence that human beings were created by God. The following is a chart used over time in an attempt to produce the *"Hominid Evidence."*

Hominid Evidence

Date	Find	Location	Evidence	Finding
1891	Java Man	Java	Skull cap, 3 teeth, thighbone, found w/ape bones	Large gibbon
1900	Neanderthal Man	West Germany	Skeletons w/large brain capacities	Complete hymen
1912	Piltown Man	Piltown, England	Fake fossils in a gravel pit	Hoax
1922	Nebraska Man	Nebraska	Tooth	Pig's tooth
1928	Peking Man	Peking	Evidence disappeared	Controversial from the beginning
1932	Ramapithecus	India	Teeth & jaw fragment	True ape; similar to orangutan
1972	Australo-pithecines	Ethiopia	40% complete skeleton	Exact ape similar to modern pygmy chimpanzee

(AQ) *After looking at the "Hominid Evidence," do you have any evidence showing that the 'ape-human" existed? If you can, how can you prove your evidence is correct?*

EVIDENCE FROM ASTRONOMY
The "Big Bang" Theory

Many Astronomers believe the universe has a **point of origin**. They believe the universe is expanding in every direction. They claim they can trace this process back to when the universe was once compressed into a primordial atom. Then this atom exploded creating this present universe.

This is the *"Big Bang"* Theory. It is supported by three discoveries:

1) An omni-directional background radiation in the universe, discovered in 1965.

2) A *"redshift"* in the radiation from more distant objects, meaning that the galaxies are rushing outward from a center point.

3) Albert Einstein's extension of his theory of relativity, which led him to conclude that the universe is both expanding and decelerating.

Here are the problems with the *"Big Bang"* Theory. Many astrophysicists do not believe it. They have three main reasons:

1) Explosions produce disorder, **not** order. *If this explosion is driving the galaxies apart, how did it first fail to drive all the atoms apart before they could come together as galaxies?*

2) This explosion cannot explain why all the planets and moons do not rotate in the same direction. Consider this: Venus, Uranus, and Pluto rotate backwards, as well as at least six of the moons in the solar system. Jupiter, Saturn, and Neptune all have moons which rotate in both directions.

3) The universe does **not** resemble the chaotic remains of an explosion.

(AQ) *What evidence do you have to show these reasons are wrong?*

The universe is an existence of **extreme order**. The planet Earth exists at exactly the right place in the universe with all the necessary conditions to produce life. For that to happen by mere chance assaults a person's common sense.

Here are a few of the many coincidences:

1) The sun;

2) The earth's rotation;

3) The earth's crust;

4) The earth's atmosphere;

5) The moon;

6) Jupiter

7) The stars;

To follow this reasoning, we must look at all seven.

The Sun

The surface of the sun is 12,000 degrees Fahrenheit. (This is very HOT.) The core is over 40 million degrees. But we are at just the right distance, 93 million miles, to heat our planet to a yearly global average of about 50 degrees.

A few degrees more or less, and life would cease to exist. – *By chance?*

(AQ) *Did YHVH create the heavens and earth or was it by evolution? If by evolution how did life exist during that time? Was this by an intelligent Designer or by chaos turning into order, destroying the* **Second Law of Thermodynamics***?*

The Earth's Rotation

The earth does 365 revelations around the sun each year. Why not 36 times? The earth rotates at a speed of over 1000 miles per hour. Every year this speed slows down by a fraction of a second. *What would happen these facts changed?* It would make our days and nights longer.

If the earth were to spin just one-tenth slower, we would experience extreme heat during the day and devastating freezes at night. If the earth were to rotate any faster, catastrophic winds would occur. Either way, life as we know it would cease.

The fact is that the Earth now rotates at a perfectly balanced speed. – *By chance?*

(AQ) *Did YHVH create the heavens and earth or was it by evolution? If by evolution how did life exist during that time? Was this by an intelligent Designer or by chaos turning into order, destroying the* **Second Law of Thermodynamics***?*

The Earth's Crust

The earth's crust is extremely thin, and beneath this crust is molten lava. If the crust was only ten feet thicker, the additional matter oxidize all the available oxygen from the air, making animal life impossible. *Was this by chance?*

It is estimated that of the ocean was 50 feet deeper or 50 feet higher that it would so upset the oxygen and nitrogen balance on earth that we could not sustain life on this planet. – *By chance?*

(AQ) *Did YHVH create the heavens and earth or was it by evolution? If by evolution how did life exist during that time? Was* *this by an intelligent Designer or by chaos turning into order, destroying* **the Second Law of Thermodynamics?**

The Earth's Orbit

The earth is moving around the sun at the perfect speed to avoid falling into the sun's heat or escaping into the coldness of space. It does not move in a circular path but more of a football-shaped orbit. This, along with the tilt of the earth's axis, which is 23 ½ degrees, creates the four seasons that make life as we know it possible. – *By chance?*

(AQ) *Did YHVH create the heavens and earth or was it by evolution? If by evolution how did life exist during that time? Was this by an intelligent Designer or by chaos turning into order, destroying the* **Second Law of Thermodynamics?**

The Earth's Atmosphere

Forty miles above the earth is a thin layer of ozone. If the ozone were to compress, it would be less than a quarter-inch thick. The atmosphere shields this planet from eight deadly solar rays and from twenty million meteors a day traveling at speeds up to twenty miles per second. *Was this done by chance?*

(AQ) *Was this by an intelligent Designer or by chaos turning into order, destroying the* **Second Law of Thermodynamics?**

The Moon

The moon orbits the earth at the perfect distance or about 240,000 miles. This creates necessary tides that clean the oceans and their shores. If the moon were to move just one-fifteenth of this distance off course, it would plunge the entire landmass of the earth under water twice a day. – *By chance?*

The moon also slows the earth's rotation to its life-sustaining pace described above; without it we would have six-hour days accompanied by nearly constant violent wind and storms.

Here is the point: If earth had experienced the slightest misstep at any point in its emergence, life would have been impossible. *Was this done by chance?*

(AQ) *Again. I ask, "Did YHVH create the heavens and earth or was it by evolution?" If by evolution how did life exist during that time? Where is your evidence?*

Jupiter

Jupiter is the fifth planet from the Sun and the largest in the Solar System. It is a giant planet with a mass one-thousandth that of the Sun, but two-and-a-half times that of all the other planets in the Solar System combined.

Jupiter is so big that 1,300 Earths could fit inside it. Jupiter's magnetic field is fourteen times as strong as earth. Because of its gravity, it absorbs asteroids and comets. It is called *"Earth's Protector."* – *By Chance?*

(AQ) *Was this by an intelligent Designer or by chaos turning into order, destroying* **the Second Law of Thermodynamics?**

The Stars

Although we can see only four thousand stars without a telescope, the Bible has declared that the number of stars are as the sand on the seashore.

Genesis 22:17: *"I will surely bless you, and I will surely multiply your offspring as the stars of heaven and as the sand that is on the seashore. And your offspring shall possess the gate of his enemies."*

Modern giant telescopes have verified as many as 10 to the 25th (10 million, billion, billion) stars in the known universe. For all the reasons above, nearly 90% of astronomers believe in God.

(AQ) *Without saying, there is an intelligent Designer, how can one explain the process of all of this, and yet not destroy the* **Second Law of Thermodynamics?**

Summary:

Here is my belief. There had to be an intelligent Designer.

Psalm 19:1 — *"The heavens declare the glory of Adonai, and the sky above proclaims His handiwork."*

Romans 1:20 — *"For His invisible attributes, namely, His eternal power and divine nature, have been clearly perceived, ever since the creation of the world, in the things that have been made. So they are without excuse."*

EVIDENCE FROM COSMOLOGY

Cosmology is the study of the origin of the cosmos (universe). One of the strongest arguments for the existence of God, the Creator, is the universe itself. This is the "Cosmological Argument." There are only three possibilities for how the universe came to be:

1) The universe created itself.

2) The universe has always existed.

3) The universe was created by an outside force that is eternal.

Let's study these three possibilities.

Option 1: The Universe Has Always Existed

In the past, scientists believed the universe had no beginning and that matter is eternal. This came into question because of the Laws of Thermodynamics. No new hydrogen is forming. If the universe is infinitely old, the stars would have burned up all the hydrogen long ago, leaving a dark, dead cosmos. Knowing the universe has a **point of origin** also makes this option unavailable.

A variation of this idea is that the expanding universe will eventually somehow reverse, collapse in on itself, and then start to expand again. In other words, we are in an infinite cycle of expansion and contraction. But this feeble attempt to preserve the "Big Bang Theory" would require the same used-up energy to somehow become usable again.

(AQ) *Can you explain this option without destroying* **the Laws of Thermodynamics?**

Option 2: The Universe Created Itself

Nothing—i.e., that which does not exist—can only produce nothing. It ALWAYS will. All evidence points to the fact that the Universe is not eternal and cannot account for its own existence.

Scientists have tried to explain the origin of the universe in terms of an exploding *"cosmic egg,"* but they have not told us where the *"egg"* came from. A cosmic egg must have come from a *"cosmic bird"* to produce or lay it. Therefore, something beyond the physical universe of space and time must have created it.

(**AQ**) *Without an intelligent Designer, can you explain how this could have happened? Where is your evidence?*

Option 3: The Universe was created by an Eternal Being

The universe could not have a beginning and be self-existent. *Why?* The very meaning of *"self-existent"* means that it has no beginning or end. Therefore, the universe has to be an effect of a cause beyond itself. Knowing the universe is non-eternal, we can deduce that something first caused it to come into existence. The only logical alternative to having a *"First Cause"* is to have *"No Cause."*

(**AQ**) *Do you have evidence for a different option?*

Below outlines the summary of the logic of the *"Cosmological Argument."* Here are the ten steps that make this argument complete:

1) Some things exist.

2) My non-existence is possible.

3) Whatever has the possibility not to exist is currently caused to exist by another existence, force, or cause.

4) There cannot be an infinite regress (or retreat) of current causes of existence.

5) Therefore a first un-caused (self-existent) source of my current existence exists.

6) This un-caused existence, force, cause, or source must be infinite (not limited by space), eternal (not limited by time), unchanging, Omniscient (all-knowing), Omnipresent (everywhere at once) Omnipotent (all-powerful), and all-perfect.

7) This infinite and eternal being is who most of us know as the Creator *"God."*

8) Therefore, the Creator *"God"* exists.

9) This Creator *"God"*, who exists, is identical to the Creator *"God"* described in the Bible.

10) Therefore, the Creator *"God"* described in the Bible exists.

There **must** be a God, the Creator.

That is why the Apostle Paul said that any person, just by looking at the universe, **has to know** by clear and common sense that the Creator *"God"* exists, and therefore that person has no excuse to deny His existence.

Romans 1:20 - *"Ever since God created the world, His invisible qualities, both His eternal power and His divine nature, have been clearly seen; they are perceived in the things that God has made. So those people have no excuse at all!"*

(AQ) *Can you prove the above logic wrong? How? "What is your evidence?*

EVIDENCE FROM REVELATION

The greatest reason we know that God exists rests in knowing He told us so. The Bible reveals these truths. (This will be later discussed in the section called *"Is the Bible True?"*)

If you wanted to tell a colony of ants you love them, the best way would be to become an ant. This way, your message would be best understood. God did exactly this. He became a man and visited Planet Earth.

To really know for sure that God does not exist, you would need to have a complete knowledge and understanding of the entire universe. You would have to be Omniscient (all-knowing), Omnipresent (everywhere at once) and Omnipotent (all-powerful). However, these are not human attributes.

Atheists challenge believers to produce God. They want believers to pull Him out of a magician's hat. Here is the problem: the evidence of God's existence is not of physical or material nature. But you can still demonstrate it in a way that will win over the jury of the mind.

The denial of God's existence based on the lack of a personal eyewitness experience would be like denying the existence of Abraham Lincoln. Just because you cannot see, touch, or talk to Him face to face today does not mean that He does not exist. You could say the same of the air that you breathe. Although you cannot see it, or touch it, you can truly know it exists.

Another example is your mind. Your mind exists; you cannot see it or touch it, yet you know it exists.

And how about Love? Joy? You cannot physically see or touch any of these with your physical senses, yet, you know, without a doubt, they exist. Just as the existence of these is evident in how they manifest themselves in our lives, so does the Creator God clearly manifest Himself in so many varied ways throughout all of Creation! The miraculous, profound, and inexplicable testimonies of Creation itself provide clear evidence of an intelligent Designer.

Many atheists, unable to prove God does *not* exist, try to put the believer on the defensive by challenging them to produce the evidence of God's existence. This evidence *does* exist, but to accept it requires a change of perception and an openness to gain that perception! If mankind is truly the product of chance or a great accident, then his final destiny is inevitably annihilation . . . or ultimately — non-existence.

Consider this:

Atheism is a philosophy without hope. Many atheists describe themselves as *"agnostic."* That also presents a problem. Here is why. The word means "no knowledge." The Latin interpretation is *"ignoramus."*

Many non-believers believe faith is belief in an invisible nothing. However, believers do not "create" God by faith. They have faith because of solid, historical evidence which clearly leads to the truth of His very existence. *"Faith is what makes real the things we hope for. It is proof of what we cannot see"* (Hebrews 11:1).

PASCAL'S WAGER

"The conduct of God, who disposes all things kindly, is to put religion into the mind by reason, and into the heart by grace. But the will to put it into the mind and heart by force and threats is not to put religion there, but terror." (*Pascal in Pensees*, p. 185)

Blaise Pascal was born June 19, 1623 and died of cancer August 19, 1662, only 39 years old. During his short life, Pascal became a great mathematician. In 1645, he invented and sold the calculating machine. It was "digital" because it operated by counting integers.

In 1654, he created "Pascal's Triangle," which calculated the probabilities of winning in gambling and today supports the study of statistics and physics.

He also invented the syringe and hydraulic press, which is a modern component of the hydraulic automobile brakes. This operates on a process known as Pascal's Law: *"Pressure applied to a confined liquid is transmitted undiminished through the liquid in all directions regardless of the area to which the pressure is applied" (www.britannica.com/sed/b/blasé-pascal/)*

Four years before the end of his life, he gave it all up because he found a question that occupied his entire thinking process: *Does God Exist?* He believed every person lives his life in this world based on his or her belief in the afterlife. Either God exists, or He does not, and each person must, from necessity, lay odds for or against Him. His conclusion became known as *"Pascal's Wager."*

The wager goes like this:

If you believe God **does** *exist, and you live your life on the basis of that belief, and then die, your choice is made.*

If you were wrong, and God did **not** *exist, you have not lost anything.*

If you were right, and God **does** *exist, you have gained everything.*

If you believe God does **not** *exist, and you live your life on the basis of that belief, and then die, your choice is made.*

*If you are right, and God does **not** exist, you have gained nothing.*

*If you are wrong, and God **does** exist, you have lost everything.*

History records Pascal's choice. *What is yours? Are you going to make the same choice as Pascal? "Choose life that you may live."* The stakes are eternal life. A person who remains an atheist/agnostic until death gains nothing . . . and stands to lose everything.

As an ex-atheist, I can tell you this: The problem is **not** an intellectual one, it is a **moral** one. We are in rebellion against our Creator God when we deny His very existence. We deny Him in spite of the many varied examples all around in creation. In these endless miraculous, profound and inexplicable testimonies, we can clearly find proof of **THE** intelligent Designer of all creation.

Many atheists come to accept the existence of God and then run into trouble with the next logical implication. It's the next chapter in our battleground: *Is the Bible true?*

IS THE BIBLE TRUE?

(AQ) Questions you ask the Atheist to make him think)

The Bible is not a science book, but where it deals with science, we have never proven it wrong. The reverse is not so. Many scientific theories have proven wrong.

THE MISSING DINOSAURS

Why doesn't the Bible mention the dinosaurs? If it tells how the earth began, you would think they would be the most visible component of a now vanished world. I would like to give you a general framework for thinking not only about this question but also other puzzling things about the Bible itself.

In the fantastic *How to Read a Book*, Mortimer Adler provides a manual on how to attack a book, how to go about understanding it. He says, *"You have to decide early on, what kind of genre the book is. If you misinterpret the type of the book, then you are lost from the very beginning and you have no chance of really understanding it."*

Imagine yourself teaching a poetry class. You read Carl Sandburg's line, *"The Fog crept in on little cat feet."* Somebody in the back of the room, raises a hand and says, "Teacher, teacher, I don't understand. How could the fog creep? It doesn't have feet, it is not a cat. This whole poem just doesn't make any sense." What would be your answer?

You would say, "You don't understand the type." There is no answer to that question, it is the wrong question. It is a bad question. You could ask if you like the imagery of the fog creeping. That's what Sandburg meant to convey, but it's entirely a different question. That's a question that makes sense for poetry. A scientific question does not work for poetry.

The bottom line is, you have to understand the type. If you misinterpret the type, you misinterpret everything. Now we must ask the great question: What kind of book is the Bible? How could we begin trying to read this book without knowing that? Here is the problem. Figuring that out is not easy.

The Torah has 613 laws, also known as instructions. That is lot of instruction. Maybe it is a law book, but it also has a lot of stories in it. What are all the stories doing in a legal treaty? That would be out of character. The Bible also has lots of philosophies in it. Could it be a philosophy book? Then why all the laws and stories? What kind of book is it?

It is a guide book. It intends to guide individuals and a nation. It explains how to develop a relationship with their neighbors as well as their God. How can you do that at the collective level if you are the nation of Israel? Or at the individual level if you are one of the people of Israel, or Gentiles connected to the *"commonwealth of Israel"? What does this guide book consists of, and what is it take to guide someone in this?*

First you need to follow and know certain instructions or laws. They are very important, but you need more than just instructions. If you say to yourself, *"all that it takes to be a good person is to follow the 613 commandments,"* that's actually not entirely true. Somebody who scrupulously keeps all the commands can still be a morally dull-witted person. *How is that possible?*

It is possible because the law (God's instructions) alone is a too narrow a discipline to completely regulate human behavior. The Bible itself accepts this. That's why it has stories. The stories are there to teach you values. The stories tell about what happened with our ancestors, the way God dealt with them, and the way they dealt with God.

These are timeless lessons that apply to us today. The Bible is not just about instructions and stories, but also larger truth. We are supposed to find a way to integrate the scriptures into our lives. For that to happen, we need to understand certain philosophical notions. The Bible talks about those ideas too. We need all of that to guide us.

If the Bible is a guide book, what does that mean? That means all its instructions (laws), stories, and philosophy will have the slant and perspective of a guide book. Any prophecy that proved relevant for generations ended up in the scriptures. Some prophecies didn't make it in; they were just locally relevant for a particular generation. *Why leave it out?* Because it doesn't guide you.

Let me show you another puzzling aspect of how the scriptures write history. You can't trust the chronological order in the Torah. Every once in a while, the Torah will actually place something second that happened first. *Why would the Torah deliberately mislead you about the chronological order of events?*

It is because it is not a history book. It is a guide book. The Bible can guide you by just transposing two different episodes with the same theme. You should understand the theme that worked over different periods of Jewish history. The Bible is going to sacrifice the history in order to guide you.

Let's come back to dinosaurs. The dinosaurs might have been around but evidently the Bible didn't consider Tyrannosaurus Rex essential to a guide to human behavior and so it left it out. If you want to learn about them, go to the American Museum of Natural History.

The Bible tells one story, and science tells another; yet ultimately it can be the same story: reality. One intends to tell you the inner workings of that reality and the other intends to guide you through it.

When you and I read this guide, make no mistake about what we are reading. We are not reading any old book. We are reading something meant to shape and to help us tackle the best way to manage our lives and relationships. Everything the Bible tells us aims to help us achieve those goals, but we need to understand the genre in order to be able to understand the messages.

INTRODUCTION

In the last chapter, we discussed the five attacks of the atheist. In review, here they are:

1) *Does God Exist?*

2) *Is the Bible True?*

3) *Is there a Resurrection?*

4) *Is Jesus God?*

5) *Is Jesus the only way to God?*

We must clarify two MAJOR points: All five questions/battlegrounds come into play through this chapter. If you are proven wrong, the atheist wins. (You need not prove the atheist wrong; <u>he must prove he is right</u>.) *How do you fight him?*

You do it with questions. Say three words – *"The Bible says. . ."* You have placed him in your battleground. If you defeat this battleground in his mind, you can win the war. If you allow the atheist to move you into other battlegrounds, you may lose.

The Bible is God's Revelation to man. It never tries to prove the existence of God; it starts in the belief that God is real. If you are a believer, it is illogical to deny the teachings of the Bible and yet believe in the God of the Bible – *Why?* It forces the questions: *How do you know if your God is real? Is your God the God of the Bible?*

Throughout history, people have rejected the true God of the Bible and sought to create their own God. Because of this, the world abounds with false religions and false gods. Many atheists choose not to believe the Bible because they confuse it with the false religions.

TEN EVIDENCES

We can offer ten major evidences as to why the Bible is true. These are:

- The Evidence of Prophecies
- The Evidence of Inspiration
- The Evidence of Infallibility
- The Evidence of Transmission
- The Evidence of Archaeology
- The Evidence of Unity
- The Evidence of Authentication
- The Evidence of Integrity
- The Evidence of Canon
- The Evidence of Preservation

Let us look at each of them.

THE EVIDENCE OF PROPHECIES

Prophecy is the prediction of future events with absolute accuracy. How do you know a prophecy is true? – If someone says it is going to happen, and it does, that is truth.

(AQ) *Do you have a problem with this statement?*

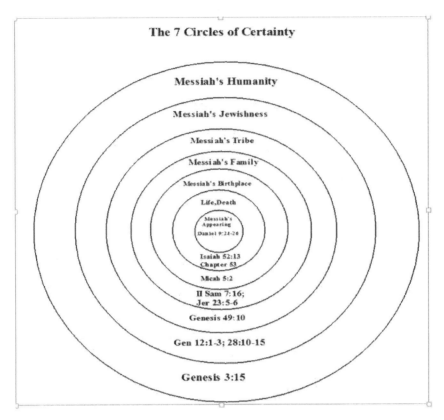

The 7 Circles of Certainty

Messiah's Humanity

Messiah's Jewishness

Messiah's Tribe

Messiah's Family

Messiah's Birthplace

Life, Death

Messiah's Appearing
Daniel 9:24-26

Isaiah 52:13
Chapter 53

Micah 5:2

II Sam 7:16;
Jer 23:5-6

Genesis 49:10

Gen 12:1-3; 28:10-15

Genesis 3:15

Apply that same meaning with these facts: There are over two thousand predictive, specific, and detailed prophecies in the Bible. The Messiah has fulfilled over 351 unique prophecies.

If one man fulfilled only 48, the probability would be 10 to the 157th power (1 with 157 zeros behind it). In their fulfillment, we can establish the divine origin of the scriptures.

(AQ) *Do you know of another man that can match these odds of probability? Where is your evidence?*

Human wisdom is unable to predict the future–only God can. The standard for the prophecy is 100% accuracy. If you find only one prophecy in the Bible wrong, you demonstrate that the Bible is not the word of God. You cannot judge a Bible prophecy on its accuracy if it has not been fulfilled YET.

God lays out His challenge in Scripture (Isaiah 46:9-11) - *"Remember what happened long ago; acknowledge that I alone am God and that there is no one else like me. From the beginning I predicted the outcome; long ago I foretold what would happen. I said that my plans would never fail, that I would do everything I intended to do. I am calling a man to come from the east; he will swoop down like a hawk and accomplish what I have planned. I have spoken, and it will be done."*

Consider this: No other major religion (Islam, Buddhism, Hindu, etc.) has even one past predictive prophecy that can be verified today, when it matters. This prophetic ability demonstrated in the Bible leaves no alternative but to believe that God himself is the author. Here are a few of selected prophecies found in the Bible.

Selected Prophecies

Civilization	Prophecy Location	Judgment	Fulfillment
Tyre	Ezekiel 26:7-21	Destruction; Never Rebuilt	By Nebuchadnezzar (in 585-573bc) and Alexander the Great (in 332bc)
Sidon	Ezekiel 28:22-23	Blood flow in streets; destruction but no extinction	By Persians in 351bc
Thebes, Egypt	Ezekiel 30:14-16	Broken up, and torn asunder	Lies in ruins; destroyed
Edom	Ezekiel 35:3-4 Isaiah 18	Perpetual desolation	Disappeared after the Fall of Jerusalem in 70ce
Gaza	Zephaniah 2:4	Abandoned, baldness	Totally disappeared, buried under sand dunes
Bethel	Jeremiah 47:5 Amos 3:14-15	Brought to nothing	The original Bethel disappeared
Babylon	Isaiah 13:19-22	Destroyed; uninhabitable	Final destruction in 4ce
Nineveh	Nahum 1-3 Zephaniah 2:13	Destroyed and desolated	Disappeared in 6th century bc
Samaria	Micah 1-6	Destroyed, foundation uncovered, would become vineyard	By Sargon, 722bc, Alexander, 331bc, and John Hyrcanus, 120bc
Capernaum	Matthew 11:20-23	Go down to Hades	Disappeared after 800ce

Isaiah 45:21 — *"Come and present your case in court; let the defendants consult one another. Who predicted long ago what would happen? Was it not I, the LORD, the God who saves his people? There is no other god."*

Religions such as Jehovah's Witnesses and Mormonism abound with false prophecies and errors, throwing serious doubt on their credibility, but the Bible has never failed in a prophecy.

Example: Cyrus would rebuild the Temple, which was still standing in its day in Jerusalem.

Isaiah 44:28 says, *"I say to Cyrus, 'You are the one who will rule for me; you will do what I want you to do: you will order that*

Jerusalem be rebuilt and that the foundations of the Temple be laid.'"

Cyrus would not even be born until 150 years later. He will release the Jews from their seventy-year captivity for them to return to Jerusalem to rebuild the then-destroyed Temple.

(AQ) *If you believe that the Bible is not real, how do you explain this evidence? Where is your evidence to substantiate your interpretation?*

THE EVIDENCE OF INSPIRATION

"Thus says the Lord" and *"God Said."* The Bible, through these statements, guarantees its own truthfulness by showing it comes from the inspiration of God. The term *"inspiration"* comes from 2 Timothy 3:16, and means, "God Breath". 2 Timothy 3:16 reads, *"**All scripture** is given by inspiration of God, and is profitable for doctrine, for reproof, for correction, for instruction in righteousness:"*

Some people teach that only some of the Bible is inspired, thus teaching that the Bible is not THE Word of God, but only contains the Word of God. But no, Timothy says, *"All Scripture."*

The writers of the New Testament recognized the authority of their message. A good example is Paul, as recorded in 1 Corinthians 14:37. *"If any man think himself to be a prophet, or spiritual, let him acknowledge that the things that I write unto you are the commandments of the Lord."*

Jesus said that every word is important. Matthew 4:4 reads, *"But he answered and said, It is written, Man shall not live by bread alone, but by every word that proceeds out of the mouth of God."*

In 2 Peter 3:15-17, Peter declares Paul's writings as scripture: *"And account that the longsuffering of our Lord is salvation; even as our beloved brother Paul also according to the wisdom given unto him hath written unto you; As also in all his epistles, speaking in them of these things; in which are some things hard to be understood, which they that are unlearned and unstable wrest, as they do also the other scriptures, unto their own destruction. Ye* **therefore***, beloved, seeing ye know these things before, beware lest ye also, being led away with the error of the wicked, fall from your own steadfastness."*

God chose to deliver His divine message through man, but He did not turn them into tape recorders. He used the personality of each writer to deliver His message. Here is an example: Luke wrote the Book of Acts. Because he was a doctor, he used medical terms which gave further insights into God's message.

The material in the Bible comes directly from God. Moses was not present at the creation, so he received the details of the creation through a supernatural way. *What does this mean?* When we read the Bible, we are reading the Word of God. Therefore, we know the Bible is true.

THE EVIDENCE OF INFALLIBILITY

It is not a theory. It is the teaching of scripture itself. It has no errors and is never wrong. In the nineteenth century, the Institute of Paris claimed to have found *"82 errors"* in the Bible, yet all of them have been solved.

Because the Bible is the Word of God, and God cannot lie (Isaiah 55:10-11, John 17:17, Titus 1:2, Hebrews 4:12), the Scriptures are completely trustworthy and free from any error.

(AQ) *If you assert that only parts of the Bible is true, how do you know is any of it is?*

What most people claim as errors are not errors but difficulties. Inconsistencies occur when people do not take the time to find out all the facts. Understand these three things:

- Lack of understanding is not an error.
- An unresolved difficulty is not an error.
- Silence from scripture is not an error.

Six major kinds of difficulties characterize those who attack the inerrancy of the Bible

- Faith Difficulties;
- Language Difficulties;
- Scientific Difficulties;
- Factual Difficulties;
- Doctrinal Difficulties;
- Ethical Difficulties;

Let's look these difficulties.

Faith Difficulties

They question the accounts in Scripture. Here are some examples: Adam and Eve, Abel, Noah, the Flood, Red Sea, Jonah, walking on water, and the Resurrection. All of these are questions of faith. Jesus confirmed the accounts of Adam and Eve, Noah, and Jonah in Matthew 12:40 and 19:4. To reject this is to reject the authority and truthfulness of Jesus.

People sometimes try to discredit what they cannot understand. Just because we do not know *how* all the miracles in the Bible occurred does not mean they did not happen.

Consider this example: Top scientists have trouble understanding the writings of Albert Einstein *How much less can finite humans understand the infinite God?* Here is what we must understand: The denial of miracles is not a question of accuracy, it is one of faith.

Language Difficulties – Figures of Speech

The Bible describes events as they appear to be. (Example – *"Sun rising and setting"*). Many would charge the Bible with errors in this matter. Why? Because the scientific knowledge states that the earth rotates. Figures of speech are not errors.

(AQ) *Are you applying different "measures" in your judgment of figures of speech between your everyday life and scripture?*

Scientific Difficulties

Some say the Bible is filled with primitive, pre-scientific views of the universe. The Bible never claimed to be a science book, but we have found no error in what it does say about science.

The Bible does not teach chemistry or biology, but it never stands in conflict with <u>VERFIED</u> science in any way. In all places that the Bible deals with scientific matters, it is completely accurate, even at times when science disagreed.

Here are a few examples:

- Roundness of the Earth (Isaiah 40:22)

- Law of Conservation of Mass and Energy (II Peter 3:7)
- Hydrological Cycle (Ecclesiastes 1:7)
- Vast number of stars (Jeremiah 33:22)
- Law of increasing entropy (Psalm 102:25-27)
- The importance of blood in the life process (Leviticus 17:11)
- Atmospheric circulation (Ecclesiastes 1:6)
- Gravitational fields (Job 26:7)

Silence about a fact is not an error.

(AQ) *If it is not in the Bible, how can you say the Bible is in error? Do you know of a scientific fact existing today that the Bible says is wrong? Where is your evidence?*

Factual Difficulties

Many difficulties in this area deal with statistics. Example: one angel speaks, according to Matthew 28:2, but its two angels in John 20:12. But Matthew's one angel does not eliminate two angels. One person may round off a number while the other may use an exact number. A closer study of the problem in this category will always reveal a logical explanation. To say that the Bible is full of error on this point has no factual basis.

Doctrinal Difficulties

We can solve this difficulty can be solved through the context of the verse. These are minor problems (Example: *faith* (Paul) vs. *works* (James)). Both Paul and James quoted Genesis 15:6 to back up their points. It reads: *"And he (Abraham) believed in the LORD; and he counted it to him for righteousness."*

Paul used the verse for the teaching of salvation (*Faith*). James used the verse for the teaching on your conduct after salvation (*Works*). We can solve these difficulties easily by examining the passage in its context along with the author's intention.

(AQ) *Are you taking your Scriptures out of context? Are you sure of your facts? What is the context of your scriptures?*

Ethical Difficulties

This is placing two Scriptures together so as to canceling each other out. Example: murder (killing the innocent) vs. capital punishment (killing the guilty). Again, you can solve these difficulties through careful study of the issues in their full context and meaning. Regardless of the kind of difficulty found, not one irreconcilable error exists in the pages of Scripture.

(AQ) *Are you taking your Scriptures out of context? If you encountered any of these difficulties, and knowing the facts, does your decision still stand?*

THE EVIDENCE OF TRANSMISSION

This is time frame of the scriptures. Because the Bible is an ancient book, some people wonder if they are reading the original message of the Bible.

The Old Testament

Scribes who copied the books of the Old Testament believed it was the Word of God. They went through great lengths to eliminate error. They counted the columns and lines on each page. They counted every line, word, and letter to find any mistakes. If the scribes discovered even one mistake, they destroyed the copy.

Example: The Dead Sea Scrolls were found in 1948. It had the complete text of Isaiah 53, written around 150 BCE. At the time, Hebrew texts rarely contained vowels. Around the year 900, a group of Hebrew scholars called Masorites added vowels to the scriptures. It became known as the *"Masoretic Text,"* from which today's Old Testament derives. In the thousand years between the texts, nothing else changed — only the vowels. Centuries passed but introduced no errors.

The New Testament:

More than 24,000 partial and complete copies are available today. No other document of antiquity can even come close. Homer's *Iliad* is second with only 643 remaining manuscripts. We have over 86,000 quotations from the early church fathers.

Consider this: If all of the Bibles on earth disappeared, we could reconstruct all but eleven verses from this material. All of this has a window of less than one hundred years after the death of Jesus. The following chart shows the timeline of the New Testament Scriptures.

The Timeline of the Acts

Acts 10	Gentiles received the Ruach Hakodush	41ce
Acts 11:30	James	45ce
Acts 15	The Jerusalem Council	50ce
Acts 15:35	Mark	50ce
Acts 18:11	I Thessalonians	52ce
Acts 18:11	II Thessalonians	53ce
Acts 19:41	I Corinthians	57ce
Acts 20:1	II Corinthians	57ce
Acts 20:3	Galatians	57-58ce
Acts 20:3	Romans	57-58ce
Acts 21	Paul completed the Nazarite Vow in Jerusalem	58ce
Acts 26:32	Matthew / Luke	60ce
Acts 28:1	Philemon	61ce
Acts 28:1	Colossians	61ce
Acts 28:16	Ephesians	63ce
Acts 28:16	Philippians	63ce

The Timeline After the Book of Acts

I Timothy	64ce
Titus	64ce
Acts	64ce
I Peter	64ce
Hebrews	65ce
II Peter	67ce
Jude	67ce
II Timothy	67ce
John	95ce
I John	95ce
II John	95ce
III John	95ce
Revelation	96ce

Buddha's sayings were not recorded until five hundred years after his death. All the books of the New Testament appeared within 70 years after Jesus' death. No other book in antiquity can compare in the number of manuscripts and the time frame between the originals and the copies. The Church possesses 100% of the New Testament. No other classical literature can make this claim.

How does this compare to other major writings? Consider the flowing chart:

COMPARISON OF MAJOR WORKS OF ANTIQUITY

(* -All from one copy)   (+ -From any one work)

Author/Work	No of Copies	When Written	Earliest Copy	Time Span
Brit Hadashah	24,000 +	40-100ce	125ce	25 yrs
Homer	653	900bc	400bc	500 yrs
Pliny the Younger (History)	7	61-113ce	850ce	750 yrs
Suetonius	8	75-160ce	950ce	800 yrs
Tacitus (Minor Works)	1	100ce	1000ce	900 yrs
Caesar	10	100-44bc	900ce	1000 yrs
Tacitus (Annals)	20	100ce	1100ce	1000 yrs
Aristophanes	10	450-385bc	900ce	1200 yrs
Plato (Tetralogies)	7	427-387bc	900ce	1200 yrs
Herodotus (History)	8	480-425bc	900ce	1300 yrs
Demosthenes	200 *	383-322bc	1100ce	1300 yrs
Thucydides (History)	8	460-400bc	900ce	1300 yrs
Sophocles	193	496-406bc	1000ce	1400 yrs
Aristotle	49+	384-322bc	1100ce	1400 yrs
Euripides	9	480-406bc	1100ce	1500 yrs
Catulius	3	54bc	1500ce	1600 yrs

(AQ) *If you still doubt that the scriptures are not accurate, please tell me where and how you base your decision. Produce your evidence.*

THE EVIDENCE OF ARCHAEOLOGY

Archaeology proves that Scripture was true. Before the nineteenth century, many facts about the historical narratives seemed unverifiable because of people, places, battles, and dates only found in the Bible. The attackers said that the writers of the Scriptures resorted to folklore, legend, and myth to validate their spiritual teaching.

The following is a chart showing charges from critics and answers from archaeology.

Past Charges by Critics	Answered by Archaeology
Moses could not have written the Torah because he lived before the invention of writing	Writing existed many centuries before Moses
Abraham's home city of Ur does not exist	Ur was discovered. One of the columns had the inscription "Abram"
The city built of solid rock called "Petra" does not exist	Petra was discovered
The "Hittites" did not exist	Hundreds of references to the Hittite civilization have been found. A person can get a Doctorate in Hittite studies at the University of Chicago
Belshazzar was not a real king of Babylon; he is not found in the records	Tablets of Babylonia describe the reign of this corgent and son of Nabonidus

An explosion of archaeological evidence has silenced the critics. We have found ancient cities and civilizations never known to exist. Over 25,000 sites have a connection to the Old Testament period. The most prominent is, again, the Dead Sea Scrolls at Qumran in 1948.

Archaeology supports the New Testament as well. Nineteenth-century critics charged that the book of Acts was a forgery from the second century. Evidence has proved them wrong. Luke was a great historian. The Pool of Bethesda, the Pool of Siloam, Jacob's well, and Pilate's residence in Jerusalem were all real places that archaeologists have found. Look at this chart of archaeological research.

Archaeological Find	Significance
Mari Tablets	Over 20000 cuneiform tablets, which date back to Abraham's time period, explains many of the patriarchal traditions of Genesis
Ebla Tablets	Over 20,000 tablets, many containing law similar to the Deuteronomy law code, The previously thought fictitious cities of the plain in Genesis 14 (Sodom, Gomorrah, Admah, Zeboiim, and Zoar) are identified
Nuzi Tablets	They detail customs of the 14th and 15th century parallel to the patriarchal accounts such as maids producing children for barren wives
Black Stele	Proved that writing and written laws existed 3 centuries before the Mosaic laws
Temple Walls of Karnak, Egypt	Signifies a 10th century bc reference to Abraham
Laws of Eshnunna (c. 1950bc) Lipit-Ishtar Code (c. 1860bc) Laws of Hammurabi (c. 1700bc)	Shows that the law codes of the Torah were not too sophisticated for that period
Ras Shamra Tablets	Provides information on Hebrew poetry
Lashish Letters	Describe Nebuchadnezzar's invasion of Judah and gives insight into the time of Jeremiah
Gedaliah Seal	Gedaliah is spoken of in 2 Kings 25:22
Cyrus Cylinder	Authenticates the biblical description of Cyrus' decree to allow the Jews to rebuild the temple in Jerusalem (2 Chron 36:23; Ezra 1:2-4)
Moabite Stone	Gives information about Omri, the 6th king of Israel
Black Obelisk of Shalmaneser III	Illustrates how Jehu, king of Israel, had to submit to the Assyrian king
Taylor Prism	Contains an Assyrian text which details Sennacherib's attack on Jerusalem during the time of Hezekiah, king of Israel

History has verified the Bible. It is no forgery. In every instance, without exception, when you can examined the archaeological evidence, you will find that the Bible is true.

(AQ) *How can the Bible be a forgery with all the physical facts verifying it? If you have other information on Biblical items*

or places that have not yet found, does that mean they do not exist?
Where is your evidence to substantiate it?

THE EVIDENCE OF UNITY

The Bible extends over 1500 years, 40 authors, 66 books, 3 languages, and different people from all walks of life in 13 countries across 3 continents. It uses history, poetry, proverbs, preaching, prophecy, parables, allegories, biography, drama, law, and letters. Yet the Bible is one vast unity (66=1). We can see the major themes of Scripture in both the Old and the New Testaments. Look at the following chart:

Themes	Tanakh	Brit Hadashah
Revelation	Torah (First 5 Books)	Revelation (Last Book)
History	Joshua - Esther	Gospels (1st 4 books)
Devotion	Job – Song of Solomon	Book of Acts
Prophecy	Isaiah - Malachi	Epistles

Is the Bible an invention of man? **No!** *Why?* Because of the time frame involved. No human conspiracy could supervise such a 1500-year project. Every author in the Bible is in perfect harmony with all the other writers in the areas of doctrine, ethics, faith, and the plan of salvation. The Bible centers on a single theme: redemption.

No human conspiracy could have occurred. The first writers had no way of knowing what others would write centuries later. So complete is the unity that the final chapters remind us not to add or subtract anything.

Revelation 22:19 reads *"And if any take anything away from the prophetic words of this book, God will take away from them their share of the fruit of the tree of life and of the Holy City, which are described in this book."*

This type of unity is a miracle of God which tells mankind about the truthfulness of the Scripture.

(AQ) *Can you name me another existing book put together this way? With these facts in mind, how can the Bible be an invention of man? If it is, where is your evidence?*

THE EVIDENCE OF AUTHENTICATION

Jesus believed in the truthfulness of the Scriptures. To reject Scripture is to reject Jesus. *Why?* Jesus used Scriptures to validate who He was (*Luke 24:27, 44; John 5*). He believed Scripture could not be broken (*John 10:35*). He believed every word and letter was important (*Matthew 5:17-19*). He believed that doctrinal error came from misunderstanding the Scriptures and rebuked the Pharisees for making their traditions equal with Scriptures (*Matthew 15:6*).

In controversies, Jesus would quote the Scriptures to end the debate (*Matthew 4:4-10, John 8:17*). He used statements like *"Search the Scriptures," "Have you not read,"* and *"It is written.*" He used the Scriptures to overcome the temptations of Satan (*Matthew* 4:4). He also verified that stories in the Old Testament were not legends or myths. Look at the following chart:

Old Testament References Acknowledged by Jesus

Creation	Mark 10:6
Adam and Eve	Mark 19:3-6
Murder of Abel	Luke 11:51
Sodom and Gomorrah	Luke 10:12
Noah	Luke 17:26-27
The Exodus	John 6:49
Miracles of Elijah	Luke 4:25-27
Abraham, Jacob and Isaac	Luke 20:37-38
Moses, author of the Torah	John 5:46-47
Isaiah wrote all of Isaiah	Matthew 4:14-16; 12:17; John 12:38-41
Daniel's Prophecies as Truth	Matthew 24:15
Jonah	Matthew 12:39-41

Could you accept the New Testament as historical but not the Old Testament? No. You cannot believe that Jesus is the Son of God and say that the Scriptures contain errors. "*That dog don't hunt.*"

The Four Possibilities

If that were true, there are only four possibilities regarding the statements of Jesus.

1) *Jesus was a fraud and lied about the Scriptures.* He was not a devious, evil liar. His entire life was one of kindness. The character of a person connects to the claims of the person.

2) *Jesus knew there were errors but covered them up to accommodate the beliefs of his day.* This is the "Accommodation Theory." Supposedly Jesus went along with erroneous views in order to present His message to listeners. The major problem with this notion: Jesus NEVER accepted false views. In the Sermon on the Mount, He used the words, *"You have heard it said . . . but I say unto you"* five times. If Jesus had taught error as truth, he would have been guilty of deception.

3) *There were errors, but Jesus was ignorant of them.* If mistaken, Jesus was a fraud. He could not have been the Son of Omniscient God and unknowingly speak untruth.

4) *The view of Jesus is correct.* Then the Bible is free from errors. No believer should reject the truthfulness of Scripture because the authority of the Messiah settles the issue.

(AQ) *Can you think of any other view that I might have missed? (If yes, produce your evidence. If not, then #4 stands.)*

THE EVIDENCE OF INTEGRITY

The Bible contains no trace of forgery. If the Bible was an invention of human minds, its characters would always have favorable portrayals. This is not the case. Scripture exposes the weakness of man and exalts the greatness of God. Even the greatest heroes of God show errors in their own judgment. A forged Bible would have tried to cover up all the negative elements.

The writers committed to telling the truth as eyewitnesses. If they had not, plenty of people were around to refute them. The time frame of the New Testament (40-95 CE) was too soon after the events for myths to develop.

The writers had nothing to gain by falsifying information; in fact, they had everything to lose.

When subjected to persecution and death, they refused to recant, and some died for the truth they wrote.

(AQ) *Why would the writers risk persecution over something for which they would not receive any material or financial benefit? Would you be willing to die for something you know to be a lie?*

THE EVIDENCE OF CANON

How do you know which books in the Bible are the right ones? A group of men did not arbitrarily select a group of books to complete the Bible. Believers have always recognized the same books as Scripture. The processes for the Old and the New Testaments differed.

Old Testament

This was developed over a period of 1100 years. When Moses produced the Torah, the Hebrews immediately identified it as inspired and authoritative. Scribes added other works deemed to have God's approval. The division was threefold: *Law, Prophets, and the Writings*. The testament became complete around 539 BCE, and all referred to it as "The Scriptures." The believers accepted these completed works in their entirety as indicated in the New Testament. (Matthew 22:29; John 10:35, 19:36; Acts 18:24; Romans 1:2; II Peter 1:20)

New Testament

This arose over a shorter time span. Because Jesus was the Promised Messiah of the Old Testament, believers accepted His words as divine and authoritative. The four books recording His earthly ministry became known as the "*Gospels.*" We may include Acts with the Gospels. Written by Luke, it reads as a sequel to his Gospel.

The Letters of the Apostles and Paul, called "*Epistles,*" circulated along with the Gospels throughout the individual congregations (Colossians 4:16; II Peter 3:16). They began with James (45 CE) and concluded with Revelation (96 CE).

These books became known as the *Canon* (Greek for *List* or *Index*).

The Three Criteria

A crisis occurred in the fourth century that caused the Church to give a formal statement on which books were "*Canon.*" In 363 CE, two Church Councils (Carthage, and Constantinople) endorsed the 27 books for the New Testament using three criteria. It must be the product of an Apostle or an eyewitness to the Apostles. It must have been quoted by the early Church fathers. Finally, it could not violate the Torah.

These tests eliminated false gospels and epistles written by heretical groups. This process of canonization ensured that today's Bible contains only the books believed to be inspired by God.

(AQ) *Do you see any problem in the way they chose the books of the Bible? (If yes, show your evidence.)*

THE EVIDENCE OF PRESERVATION

The Bible is the most persecuted book in all of history. For two thousand years, people have made every possible effort to undermine the authority of the Bible, including emperors, kings, popes, and scholars. It endured attacks by intellectual, political, philosophical, scientific, and physical forces.

Some rulers, like Roman Emperor Diocletian in 303 CE, made it a capital offense to have a Bible.

Every family caught with a Bible would die. His soldiers burned every Bible they found and killed thousands of believers. So successful was he that he thought he had brought an end to the Bible. He erected a column inscribed with the words: *"The Name of Christians has been extinguished"* in Latin. His efforts failed. Within ten years, Christianity would become the official religion of the Roman Empire.

Great thinkers throughout the centuries tried to destroy the Bible. Allow me to present two examples:

Example #1: The eighteenth-century French philosopher *Voltaire*. He attacked it so strongly that he predicted that within fifty years it would be forgotten. Fifty years after his death, the Geneva Bible Society would use his printing press and home to produce Bibles.

Example #2: *Thomas Paine*. Two centuries ago, Thomas Paine attacked the Bible with *The Age of Reason*. He believed his argument was powerful enough to dispose of the Bible permanently. He said that within a few years, the Bible would be out of print. Two hundred years later, his book is out of print and the Bible remains the all-time seller.

(AQ) *If the Bible was a man, how would you regard a man who was hanged, poisoned, drowned, burned, shot, and yet would not die? – Would you regard that man as superhuman?*

This is how we should view the Bible: It is a supernatural book. It has been persecuted, mocked, burned, and torn to pieces, yet never destroyed. If this was the work of man, it would have perished a long time ago. *Why?* The average book only survives about 20 years. The Bible has survived over 1800 years, translated into over 1700 languages. Given that few speak Latin or Aramaic today, you could say it has outlasted some of its own language.

(AQ) *What other book has gone through such resistance and still survived?*

God Himself promises the perseverance of His word in Matthew 24:35 – *"Heaven and earth will pass away, but my words will never pass away."*

Isaiah wrote these words over 2500 years ago: *"Grass withers and flowers fade away, when the LORD's breath blows on them, but the word of our God will stand forever"* (Isaiah 40:8).

Why has the Bible generated so much hatred? The Bible reveals the guilt of humanity and holds us accountable for our sins. The problem most people have with the Bible is not its alleged inaccuracies. They oppose its teachings on how a sinful man is reconciled to a holy God. Most people have not rejected the Bible on intellectual grounds, but spiritual ones. To reject the Bible without demonstrating it to be false is a very unwise decision.

(NOTE: If the atheist can surrender to this battle and accept the Bible as true, you will destroy the rest of his battlegrounds. Then God, through you, has won the war for his soul.)

(AQ) *Is your life straight? If you still believe the Bible is not true, how do you substantiate your judgment" Where is your evidence?*

As an atheist, the next chapter was a major part of my battleground. This is what turned me into an atheist. It ultimately changed my life twice—once going in and another coming out. Again, prepare your spiritual arrows as we go into *"Is there a Resurrection?"*

IS THERE A RESURRECTION?

(AG) Questions you ask the Atheist to make him think)

INTRODUCTION-REVIEW

This a small review of what we covered so far

The Five Attacks of the Atheist:

1) *Does God Exist?*

2) *Is the Bible True?*

3) *Is there a Resurrection?*

4) *Is Jesus God?*

5) *Is Jesus the only way to God?*

Two MAJOR Points:

1) All five Questions/Battlegrounds hinge upon #2 (If we are proven wrong, the atheist wins)

2) It is not up to you to prove the Atheist wrong, <u>He must prove he is right</u>. *With these two points in mind, how do you fight him?* <u>With questions.</u>

(**AG**) *Are you a "Seeker of the Truth?" OR are you a closed-minded skeptic?*

(This teaching covers the third Battlefield of the Atheist – *"Is there a Resurrection"*)

FIRST FRUITS AND THE RESURRECTION

Leviticus 23:10 reads, *"Speak to the sons of Israel and say to them, 'When you enter the land which I am going to give to you and reap its harvest, then you shall bring in the sheaf of the* <u>first fruits</u> *of your harvest to the priest."*

"First Fruits" refers to the first portion of the harvest which is given to God. They are:

- The first to come in time;
- A pledge or hope of the greater harvest to follow;
- Specially dedicated to God.

The Hebrews also considered the firstborn, whether human or beast, as God's special possession and a type of first fruit.

Exodus 22:29-30 reads, *"Give Me the offerings from your grain, your wine, and your olive oil when they are due. Give Me your first-born sons. Give Me the first-born of your cattle and your sheep. Let the first-born male stay with its mother for seven days, and on the eighth day offer it to Me."*

Exodus 34:19-20 reads, *"Every first-born son and first-born male domestic animal belongs to Me, but you are to buy back every first-born donkey by offering a lamb in its place. If you do not buy it back, break its neck. Buy back every first-born son. No one is to appear before Me without an offering."*

All believers are especially dedicated to God in the manner of first fruits. James 1:18 reads, *"Of His own will He brought us forth by the word of truth, that we might be a kind of first fruits of His creatures."* We all, Jew and Gentile, belong to God.

Jeremiah 2:3 describes Israel as the *"first fruits of God's harvest."* Israel was to be a pledge of a greater harvest inasmuch of God's redemption and would witness this redemption to the nations so they too might come to know the God of Israel.

God also promised that we will be raised from the dead. In Romans 8:23, Paul says that as redeemed people we possess the *"first fruits of the Spirit."* The measure of the Holy Spirit we have now will be in greater measure in the age to come.

The Veil of the Temple

Matthew 27:51-54 reads, *"Then, behold, the veil of the temple was torn in two from top to bottom; and the earth quaked, and the rocks were split, and the graves were opened; and many bodies of the believers who had fallen asleep were raised; and coming out of the graves after His resurrection, they went into the holy city and appeared to many. So when the centurion and those with him, who were guarding Jesus, saw the earthquake and the things that had happened, they feared greatly, saying, 'Truly this was the Son of God!'"*

Let's compare these verses with the Jewish burial practices in Jerusalem during the Second Temple period and then ask two questions:

- *What happened to these resurrected believers?*
- *What is the prophetic significance of the veil of the Temple being torn in two from top to bottom and the believers being resurrected?*

Second Temple Burial Practices

A Jewish person who died in Jerusalem during this time was usually buried before sundown, or at least within 24 hours of death. The body was taken to the family's rock-cut tomb, where it was washed and wrapped in burial shrouds. It was then either placed in a burial niche called a *kok* (*kokim* plural) located in the tomb, or on a bench in the tomb called an *arcosolia*. There, the body would decay.

The family would return to their home and have a seven-day period of intense mourning called *shiva*. They would turn over the bed of the dead person and smash any pottery vessels in the house because they were ritually defiled by the dead. The men would not shave for the week.

The extended family and friends would visit and console the bereaved family on the loss of their loved one.

After the week was over, the immediate family had a less intense period of mourning for thirty days, called *sholshim*.

On the one-year anniversary of the individual's death, the family returned to the burial cave, gathered the bones of the dead, anointed them with olive oil and wine, and then placed them in a bone box called an ossuary. This ossuary was then placed elsewhere in the tomb. The rock-cut tombs containing the dead were buried were outside the city walls of Jerusalem. From these tombs the resurrected believers came forth.

Resurrection of the Believers

The gospel of Matthew the only gospel to record the account of the opening of the tombs and the believers being resurrected.

Matthew, the author is this Gospel, was also called Levi. He was a scribe and a tax collector. He wrote this book primarily to the Jewish people to demonstrate that the Lord Jesus was the fulfillment of all that the Hebrew prophets wrote and spoke about concerning their Messiah, the Son of

God. The key word in the book is *"fulfilled."* It usually meant *"proved the truth of words spoken or written by the prophets."*

Verbatim verses of the Hebrew Scriptures appear continually in this gospel. Matthew assumes his readers have a Jewish mindset and know the Torah and rabbinic theology. Therefore, he does not explain some things. Readers of Scriptures also need to know this material in order to fully appreciate the words of this gospel. *Why?* Because it is a Jewish book.

Note that the resurrection of the Hebrew believers occurred when Jesus rose from the dead. Chronologically, that would have occurred by Sunday morning. *What was going on in Jerusalem on Sunday morning of Passover week?* For this, we need to turn to the Hebrew Scriptures.

The Omer of the First Fruits

The LORD has a divinely ordained agricultural / religious calendar that began in the month of Aviv, also known as Nisan. The *"Feasts of the LORD"* are in Leviticus 23. This calendar is also God's prophetic program of redemption for individuals as well as nationally, for all Israel. The morning after the Shabbat that followed the Passover was the harvesting of the Omer of the first fruits of the barley harvest as recorded in Leviticus 23:9-14.

In the first century BCE and early first century CE, a debate raged between the Pharisees and the Sadducees concerning the timing of this event. The Pharisees understood Shabbat in verse 11 as being a Festival Day, the first Day of Passover. The Sadducees, who controlled the services of the Temple, and rejected the oral law and traditions of the Pharisees, understood the phrase in verse 11, *"the morrow after the Sabbath,"* in a literal sense — i.e., the day following the first Shabbat after the Passover (Sunday morning).

The Lord gave Moses the instructions concerning the Feasts. These feasts had an agricultural and religious purpose to teach the people to trust the Lord, and Him only, in their daily lives throughout the year. But they also had a prophetic purpose concerning God's program of redemption. The first two feasts are Passover (*Pasach*) and Unleavened Bread (Leviticus 23:4-8).

Paul referenced Passover and Unleavened Bread in a discussion on congregational issues, saying: *"Therefore purge out the old leaven, that you may be a new lump, since you truly are unleavened. For indeed the Messiah, our Passover, was sacrificed for us. Therefore let us keep the feast, not with old leaven, nor with the leaven of malice and wickedness, but with the unleavened bread of sincerity and truth"* (1 Corinthians 5:7-8).

Also Peter alludes to the Passover Lamb when he describes the redemption of Jesus purchased *"with the precious blood of the Messiah, as of a lamb without blemish and without spot"* (1 Peter 1:19; cf. Exodus 12:5; Leviticus 22:18-20). This is the Lamb of which John the Baptist spoke. He saw Jesus coming toward him at Bethany beyond the Jordan and said, *"Behold! The Lamb of God who takes away the sin of the world!"* (John 1:29). Jesus is the fulfillment of the Feast of Passover and Unleavened Bread.

But what about the Omer (sheaf) of the first fruits of the barley harvest? Paul gives a hint as to its meaning when he wrote to the congregation at Corinth about the resurrection of the Messiah. He stated: *"But now the Messiah is risen from the dead, and has become the first fruits of those who have fallen asleep"* and he went on to say, *"But each one in his own order: the Messiah the first fruits, afterwards those who are Messiah's at His coming"* (1 Corinthians 15:20, 23).

If you are a believer, use your sanctified imagination for a minute. On the first day of the week, a group of women went out the Gennath Gate (Garden Gate) to the tomb of Joseph of Arimathea in order to anoint the body of Jesus.

Other groups of people also left the city of Jerusalem early that morning. These people followed the Sadducee tradition concerning the cutting of the Omer of barley. They were heading toward the barley fields in the Valley of Rephaim, west of Jerusalem, following Isaiah 17:5.

Can you imagine them leaving the gates of the city with sickle in hand and baskets on their shoulders, and having a festive attitude as they went to harvest the Omer?

As they walked to the barley fields, they saw some people approaching them, heading toward Jerusalem. One was their previously dead Uncle Eliyahu, another was Grandpa Akiva, as well as cousins Yonah, Elisheva and Batya, all dressed in tattered burial shrouds! Imagine their shock. *"Hey, Gramp, what are you doing here? We buried you twenty years ago!"* This experience went against their theology. *Why?* It was because the Sadducees did not believe in the resurrection of the body (Acts 23:8)!

What Happened to these Resurrected Believers? There are three possibilities.

The **first** possibility is they are still alive today.

I've met a lot of people, but I have never met anybody that was two thousand years old. (I'll assume Mel Brooks was just doing a comedy routine.)

The **second** possibility is that they died again.

We have no Scriptural guarantee, nor Jewish or Christian traditions saying they died again.

The **third** possibility is that they ascended into Heaven with Jesus forty days after His, and their resurrection. I believe this one is correct

The Ascension of Jesus

After Jesus gives another commission to His disciples (Acts 1:8), Luke records: *"Now when He had spoken these things, while they watched, He was taken up, and **a cloud** received Him out of their sight. And while they looked steadfastly toward heaven as He went up, behold, two men stood by them in white apparel, who also said, 'Men of Galilee, why do you stand gazing up into heaven? This same Jesus, who was taken up from you into heaven, will so come in like manner as you saw Him go into heaven.'"* (Acts 1:9-11)

Notice several things in this passage. **First**, *"a cloud"* received Him out of their sight. Most commentators would state that when Jesus ascended, He disappeared into a cloud, a vaporous mass. But Luke may be using this word in another way.

Second, when the Apostle Paul describes the return of the Lord Jesus in the air for His believers, he states, *"Then we who are alive and remain shall be caught up together with them in the clouds to meet the Lord in the air. And thus we shall always be with the Lord."* (1 Thessalonians 4:17)

Note that in the Greek text, there is no definite article before *"clouds."* So a better translation would be that the living believers shall be caught up *"in clouds"* to meet the Jesus in the air. At that time there would be a cloud of believers over every continent.

I believe Luke is using the word *"clouds"* in this manner, as a collection of believers. Thus, the cloud that received Jesus above the Mount of Olives was a cloud of the believers resurrected in Jerusalem along with Jesus. This was the first fruits of a greater harvest to come and the prophetic point of the Feast of the LORD. Here is why.

The Israelites were to bring the first fruits of the barley harvest to the Temple, and the priest would wave the *Omer* (sheaf) before the LORD, acknowledge His provision for the harvest, and trust Him for the full harvest in the months to come.

In the prophetic analogy, the priest would not wave just one stalk (Jesus) before the LORD, but a sheaf (Jesus and the people resurrected at the same time). This fulfilled the prophetic aspect of the Feast of First Fruits and what Paul wrote, *"Messiah, risen from the dead, has become the first fruits of those who have fallen asleep."*

Believers are described as the ones having the *"first fruits of the Spirit."* This is a declaration that the Holy Spirit is *"the first fruits"* (*aparchēn*) of God's work of salvation and re-creation in believers. The believers' spirits have been resurrected from the dead and are now spiritually alive in the Messiah.

Believers are therefore awaiting the ultimate fulfillment of their sanctification, which is the redemption of their mortal (doomed to death) physical bodies.

Jesus, the Messiah, has already received His glorified body and is the first fruits of those who believe in Him. And now believers groan together with all of creation in the hope of receiving our immortal bodies and becoming fully conformed to the image of Messiah (Romans 8:29).

Notice also the words of the two men in white apparel, most likely angelic beings: *"This same Jesus, who was taken up from you into heaven, will so come in like manner as you saw Him go into Heaven"* (Acts 1:11).

When Jesus returns to earth with His believers at His revelation as the King of Kings, and Lord of Lords, John states that *"He is coming with clouds (of believers), and every eye shall see Him, even they who pierced Him. And all the tribes of the earth will mourn because of Him. Even so, Amen"* (Revelation 1:9; cf. Revelation 19:11-16).

The Crucifixion

Remember those Sadducees in Jerusalem who were amazed at seeing their resurrected relatives? They were confused about what was happening.

The last question that we need to address: *"What is the significance of the veil of the Temple tearing in two and the believers being resurrected?"* In order to answer this question, we must examine the larger context of the crucifixion in Matthew's gospel. In verses 39-44, two groups of people mock Jesus because of His claim to be the Son of God.

"And those who passed by blasphemed Him, wagging their heads and saying, 'You who destroy the temple and build it in three days, save Yourself! If You are the Son of God come down from the cross'" (Matthew 27:39-40).

This taunt of *"**If** You are the Son of God"* echoes the words Satan used when he tested Jesus from the pinnacle of the Temple (Matthew 4:6).

This **first group** of mockers also invoked the testimony of the false witnesses at Jesus' trial before the Sanhedrin. The false witnesses said, *"This fellow said, 'I am able to destroy the temple of God and to build it in three days'"* (Matthew 26:61).

They misconstrued Jesus because He was speaking of the temple of his body (John 2:19-21). Nevertheless, the high priest put Jesus under oath and said, *"Tell us if You are the Christ, the Son of God!"* Jesus acknowledged, *"It is as you said"* (Matthew 26:63-64).

The **second group**, the chief priests, scribes and elders, mocked Him thus:

"He saved others; Himself He cannot save. If He is the King of Israel, let Him now come down from the cross, and we will believe Him. He trusted in God; let Him deliver Him now if He will have Him; for He said, 'I am the Son of God'" (Matthew 27:42-43).

This group, predominately Sadducees, mocked His claim to be the Son of God. They also invoked Psalm 22:8: *"He trusted in the LORD, let Him rescue Him; Let Him deliver Him, since He delights in Him."* Unknowingly, they fulfilled the words of verse 7 as well, *"All those who see Me ridicule Me; they shoot out the lips, they shake the head, saying, 'He trusted in the LORD.'"*

The death of the Messiah turns the tables on the mockers. God the Father had said of His Son at His baptism, *"This is My beloved Son, in whom I am well pleased"* (Matthew 3:17). And again at the Transfiguration, *"This is My beloved Son, in whom I am well pleased. Hear Him"* (Matthew 17:5).

Jesus hung suspended between Heaven and earth while there darkness descended over the earth for three hours. At the ninth hour, He cried out with a loud voice, in Hebrew, *"My God, My God, why have You forsaken Me"* (Psalm. 22:1)? This was the opening lines of Psalm 22, also invoked by the chief priests, scribes and elders. Now Jesus invokes it.

A Jewish person during the Second Temple period would have most, if not all, of the psalms memorized. The answer to Jesus' question was obvious. Psalm 22:3 states, *"But You are holy!"*

Because of God's holiness, the Father could not look upon His Son as He became sin for us and took all the sins of all humanity upon Himself (2 Corinthians 5:21; 1 John 2:2), so darkness covered the earth. Matthew records that *"Jesus cried out again with a loud voice, and yielded up His spirit."* (Matthew 27:50) John reveals these words: *"It is finished!"* (John 19:30). After paying the full price for all sin, Jesus voluntarily gave up His life (John 10:11-18).

The Two Signs

In a Jewish court of law, an established fact requires two or more witnesses (Deuteronomy 17:6-7; 19:15). God the Father gave two signs to the nation of Israel in order to vindicate His Son.

The **first sign** was at His death. The veil of the Temple tore from top to bottom. Only God could do this, making it a divine sign. Its message was twofold:

The **negative aspect** was that God was finished with the corrupt priesthood, mostly controlled by the Sadducees.

The **positive aspect** was it showed that Jesus had paid for all sin and the way to God was open to all, both Jews and Gentiles. This message was clear to the centurion and his men guarding the tomb of Jesus. They saw all that transpired — the darkness and the earthquake — and feared greatly. The centurion said, *"Truly this was the Son of God"* (Matthew27:54)!

This was also the beginning of the fulfillment of Psalm 22:27-28: *"All the ends of the world shall remember and turn to the LORD, and all the families of the nations shall worship before You. For the kingdom is the LORD's, and He rules over the nations."*

It also affirms the creed that Paul states at the beginning of the book of Romans: *"Concerning His Son, who was born of the Seed of David according to the flesh, and declared to be the Son of God with power according to the Spirit of holiness, by the resurrection from the dead. Jesus Christ our Lord."* (Romans1:3-4)

Matthew recorded the Gentiles' expression of faith in Jesus as the Son of God. This was to provoke Israel to jealousy (Romans 11:11-14). A few years later, Luke records that *"a great many of the priests were obedient to the faith."* (Acts 6:7) *Had they thought through the theological implications of the veil being rent?*

The **second sign** was at the resurrection of Jesus, many believers rose from the dead. This showed the Sadducees the bodily resurrection was real. The Lord prophesied through Ezekiel's vision of the valley of dry bones that these were the whole House of Israel. He said of them:

"Behold, O My people, I will open your graves and cause you to come up from your graves, and bring you into the Land of Israel. Then you shall know that I am the LORD, when I have opened your graves, O My people, and brought you up from your graves. I will put My Spirit in you, and you shall live, and I will place you in your own land. Then you shall know that I, the LORD, have spoken it and performed it" (Ezekiel 37:12-14).

The believers that were raised were the first fruits of a greater harvest/resurrection to come. Ezekiel also described the resurrection of those who died outside the Land of Israel. At the end of days, those also will be resurrected and brought back into the Land.

THE HISTORY OF FIRST FRUITS

Israel's Feast of First Fruits was an ancient holy day devoted to first things.

The Meaning

First Fruits marked the beginning of the cereal grain harvests in Israel. Barley was the first grain to ripen of those sown in the winter months. For First Fruits, farmers would harvest a sheaf of barley and bring it to the Temple as a thanksgiving offering to the Lord for the harvest.

The First Fruits was representative of the barley harvest as a whole and served as a pledge or guarantee that the remainder of the harvest would arrive in the days that followed.

Consider this: A sheaf is symbolic of a human being. Remember the dream of Joseph?

The Preparation

As the barley grows, the Hebrews marked the first growth with a cord around it. It became known as the *"first fruits."*

At sundown, marking the beginning of Nisan 16, a three-man team from the Sanhedrin, with sickles in hand, leads a progression to the special barley field across the Kidron Valley in the Ashes Valley.

At the valley, this three-man team would ask a series of questions allowing them to cut the barley.

- "Has the sun set?"
- "Do I cut?"
- "With this sickle?"
- "Into this basket?"
- "On this Sabbath?"

After getting the verification, they cut the marked sheaves until obtaining one ephah of barley (about 2/3 bushel).

In the Temple court, the grain was threshed with rods to prevent injury to the barley corns. It would be parched over an open flame and winnowed in the wind to remove the chaff. The barley was then milled and sifted intensely fine.

According to the Talmud (Menahot 8:2), this process continued until one of the Temple inspectors could plunge his hands into the flour and remove them without any flour sticking to their hands. *What does the beating, crushing and grinding of the barley grain into flour mean?*

The barley sheaf was marked in the field and then cut, which points to Jesus first being marked for sacrifice and then cut off or killed. Isaiah prophesied this would happen when he predicted that the right arm redeemer of YHVH

(*Isaiah* 53:1) would first grow up like a tender plant out of the dry ground (*Isaiah* 53:2).

The Jews, when seeking barley to be harvested for the wave sheaf offering, insisted that it had grown naturally without the benefit of artificial watering or manuring.

Isaiah refers to Jesus as a *"tender plant"* (*Isaiah* 53:2). This is a picture of the barley in its *abiv* or *green-in-the-ear* state. This is why the priests had to roast the barley in fire before they could grind it. Though the barley was substantive, the ear still contained moisture.

To grind even slightly moist grain will clog up the grinding stones so that they cannot function. They roasted the grain get it completely moisture free.

Isaiah then prophesied that the Messiah would be *"cut off from the land of the living"* (*Isaiah* 53:8), even as the barley was cut off with a sickle from the dry land where it had grown to fruition.

The Presentation

The temple process is as follows: At 9 a.m. on Nisan 16, the first fruits were presented before the Lord. One Omar (about five pints) of the barley flour was mixed with a quarter-pint of Olive Oil, and a small of frankincense was sprinkled on it. This became the first fruits offering.

The priest waved it before the Lord in accordance with Leviticus 23:11-13 and burned a small amount upon the altar. The remainder went to the Levites.

Leviticus 23:11-13 says, *"And he shall wave the sheaf before the LORD, to be accepted for you: on the morrow after the Sabbath the priest shall wave it. And ye shall offer that day when ye wave the sheaf a he lamb without blemish of the first year for a burnt offering unto the LORD. And the meat offering thereof shall be two tenth deals of fine flour mingled with oil, an offering made by fire unto the LORD for a sweet savour: and the drink offering thereof shall be of wine, the fourth part of a hin."*

What is the Family Process? First fruits was a national observance, but each family brought their first fruits offering to the temple. They also did the same process as the Levites.

Inside the temple gates, Levitical choirs led the worship music with Psalm 30: *"I will extol You, O Lord, for you have lifted me up. And have not let my foes rejoice over me..."* This scene continues throughout the day.

In the Court of the Israelites, each family would present their animal and barley offerings to the priest. They would watch as the priest prepared these offerings according to Leviticus 1:14-17 and placed the parts on the altar.

Standing face to face with the priest, they would repeat the First Fruits prayer: *"I declare today to the Lord your God that I have come to the country which the Lord swore to our fathers to give us."*

He would than hand the basket containing the first fruits of barley to the priest. The priest would place his hand under the basket and slowly wave it before the Lord. At this point, the farmer would continue the first fruits prayer:

"My father was a Syrian, about to parish, and he went down to Egypt and dwelt there, few in number: and there he became a nation, great, mighty, and populous. He has brought us to this place and has given us this land. 'A land flowing with milk and honey' and now, behold I have brought the first fruits of the land which you, O Lord, have given me." (Deuteronomy 26:5, 9-10)

With the thanksgiving prayer complete, the priest set the basket in front of the altar and cast a handful of the grain on the fire. The farmer would return to the outer court to rejoin his family. The commandments for the holy day were now fulfilled.

FIRST FRUITS IN THE NEW TESTAMENT
The Scriptures

In the New Testament, human beings become First Fruits. Romans 16:5 says, *"Likewise greet the church that is in their house. Salute my well beloved Epaenetus, who is the first fruits of Achaia unto the Messiah."*

1 Corinthians 16:15 says, *"I beseech you, brethren, (ye know the house of Stephanas, that it is the <u>first fruits</u> of Achaia, and that they have addicted themselves to the ministry of the believers,"*

Romans 11:16 says, *"For if the first fruit be holy, the lump is also holy: and if the root be holy, so are the branches."*

Paul used the process of the dough in the making of bread. By this He meant that if God chose and accepted first fruit (the Patriarchs), then the whole lump (Israel) belonged to Him. Therefore he could say in Romans 11:2 (same chapter), *"God has not cast away His people."*

James 1:18 says, *"Of his own will begat he us with the word of truth, that we should be a kind of <u>first fruits</u> of his creatures."*

And then Romans 8:23 says, *"And not only they, but ourselves also, which have the <u>first fruits</u> of the Spirit, even we ourselves groan within ourselves, waiting for the adoption, to wit, the redemption of our body."*

This verse tells us the *"first fruits of the Spirit"* is Salvation.

The indwelling of the Spirit of God is the guarantee, or pledge, of a final redemption. Our bodies will be glorified and creation redeemed from the curse.

Also consider Revelation 14:4 (The 144,000):*"These are they which were not defiled with women; for they are virgins. These are they which follow the Lamb whithersoever he goeth.*

These were redeemed from among men, being <u>the first fruits unto</u> <u>God and to the Lamb</u>.*"*

The 144,000 are the first fruits of a future harvest within the Nation of Israel. It is God's pledge (first fruit) that He has not cast off His people, thereby fulfilling the Scripture: *"And all Israel will be saved"* (Romans 11:26).

The Fulfillment

1 Corinthians 15:20— *"But now is the Messiah risen from the dead, and* <u>become the first fruits</u> *of them that slept."*

This forces a question: *How was the Messiah our first fruits?* 1 Corinthians 15:22-24 answers this: *"For as in Adam all die, even so in the Messiah shall all be made alive. But every man in his own order: Messiah the first fruits; afterward they that are the Messiah's at his coming. Then cometh the end, when he shall have delivered up the kingdom to God, even the Father; when he shall have put down all rule and all authority and power."*

The resurrection of Jesus is the guarantee and the beginning (*first fruits*) of the final harvest, or resurrection, of all mankind.

The Messiah fulfilled the prophetic meaning of this holy day by rising from the dead to become the first fruits of the resurrection, and He did it on the very day of first fruits.

The Bible clearly teaches life after death. All will be resurrected. Only the quality of that eternal existence remains in question. Daniel 12:2 prophesies, *"And many of those who sleep in the dust of the earth shall awake. Some to everlasting life. Some to shame and everlasting contempt."*

Jesus further explained Daniel in John 5:28-29, *"Marvel not at this: for the hour is coming, in the which all that are in the graves shall hear his voice, And shall come forth; they that have done good, unto the resurrection of life; and they that have done evil, unto the resurrection of damnation."*

Just as the harvest has two parts, the wheat or barley and the chaff, there will be two parts to the final harvest.

Some will inherit eternal life and dwell in the house of the Lord forever. Others will inherit eternal separation from God, confined forever to the lake of fire.

Jesus provided the ironclad guarantee when He rose from the dead. It will happen because, as recorded in 1 Corinthians 15:20, *"But now is the Messiah risen from the dead, and become the first fruits of them who have fallen asleep."*

BUT the fact is, there is the Resurrection.

This feast had its fulfillment in the Resurrection of Jesus. 1 Corinthians 15:3-4 says, *"For I delivered to you as of FIRST IMPORTANCE which I also received, that the Messiah died for our sins according to the scriptures, and that He was buried, and that He was raised on the third day* according to the scriptures."

PAUL'S SEVEN PILLARS

You must apply the <u>seven pillars</u> of Paul's theology as you study his letters. Otherwise, you are taking Scripture out of its context to make it fit a doctrine you cannot prove in the Bible.

1. Paul was a Pharisee–He never changed from one religion to another.

2. Paul's view of the Torah was always positive.

3. Paul's calling mission was to the Gentiles, yet he remained an orthodox Jew.

4. Love must characterize the believer's life of ministry to others

5. The grace of God reveals itself through Jesus, the Messiah

6. The resurrection of Jesus is the First Fruit of the general Resurrection

7. Jesus is coming again to complete the work of Redemption. All must be prepared for the Day of Judgment.

Many people have misunderstood the Resurrection and what it means.

DEFINING THE CONCEPT

To continue with our identification, we must understand three concepts.

1. *Resuscitation*: Vital signs stop then restart
2. *Reincarnation*: Soul passes to another body at death
3. *Resurrection*: Physical body returns to life, incorruptible

As an atheist, I have used the first two concepts, Resuscitation and Reincarnation, to try to explain what happened with Jesus. I flatly rejected the third concept, Resurrection. If you would apply the historical evidence in the case of Jesus, though, it's the only one that will stand.

THE HISTORICAL FACTS

As an EX-atheist, I have assembled nine historical facts you must try to explain to reject the Resurrection.

1) Jesus died by means of crucifixion.
2) Jesus' body was placed in a guarded tomb.
3) The disciples were shattered that their Messiah was dead. They lost all hope and did not expect a Resurrection.
4) They found the tomb of Jesus empty on the third day.

5) Eyewitnesses reported the bodily appearance of Jesus on several occasions.

6) The faith of the disciples radically transformed into a bold belief in the Resurrection. They willingly sacrificed their lives for the cause of their faith.

7) The proclamation of the Resurrection began in Jerusalem, where Jesus was crucified.

8) The Messianic Movement began on the day of the Resurrection.

9) Jesus appeared to James and Paul, both of whom experienced a change of heart as a result.

THE RESURRECTION CHALLENGE

Does it matter that the Resurrection really happened? **YES**. *Why?* If we show that the Resurrection happened, then His claims are true. If it did not happen, and we believe it, we are fools (*1 Corinthians 15:14-19*).

(Note: These are the steps of an atheist. As an atheist, I took all of the steps.)

The Seven Steps Downward – *1 Corinthians 15:13-19*

v. 13 *The Messiah is not risen.*

v. 14 *Our preaching is in vain, and we are wasting our time.*

v. 15 *We are declared liars.*

v. 17 *Your faith is worthless.*

v. 17 *You are still in your sins.*

v. 18 *Those who have died in the Messiah have perished.*

v .19 *We who are alive are to be pitied.*

BUT the Resurrection is a fact. *What does this mean?* The Resurrection of the Messiah is the Constitution, Bill of Rights, and the Declaration of Independence of the Messianic Faith.

The Resurrection is the key to evaluating Jesus' claims. It is God's *"Amen"* to Jesus as the only way to salvation. If the Resurrection is true, then any other religion claiming a different way to God is false.

(AQ) *If you become convinced that the Resurrection actually took place, would you become a believer in Jesus?*

THE RESURRECTION EVIDENCE

We can use these six evidences can show the Resurrection happened historically.

1) *The Evidence of Prophecy*
2) *The Evidence of the Empty Tomb*
3) *The Evidence from Eyewitnesses*
4) *The Evidence of the Transformation of the Disciples*
5) *The Evidence of Jesus being worshiped as God*
6) *The Evidence of the creation of the Messianic Believers (Church?)*

THE EVIDENCE OF PROPHECY

1) *The Old Testament abounds with its prophecies.* (*Genesis 3:15; Psalm 2:7; Psalm 16:9-11; Psalm 22:14-15; Psalm 40:1-3; Psalm 110:1; Isaiah 53:9-12; Hosea 5 and 6; Zechariah 12:10*)

Paul writes in 1 Corinthians 15:3-4, *"For I delivered to you as of first importance what I also received, that Christ died for our sins* <u>according to the Scriptures</u>, *and that He was buried, and that He was raised on the third day* <u>according to the Scriptures.</u>*"*

2) *Jesus prophesied His own death and resurrection.* (*Matthew 12:38-42; Matthew 16:21; Matthew 17:9, 23; Matthew 20:19; Mark 14:28; Luke 9:22; John 2:19*)

He staked His entire ministry on the single fact that He would rise from the dead on the third day.

Matthew 12:39-40 *"But He answered and said to them, "An evil and adulterous generation craves for a sign; and yet no sign will be given to it but the sign of Jonah the prophet; for just as Jonah was three days and three nights in the belly of the sea monster, so will the Son of Man be three days and three nights in the heart of the earth."*

This is a total of 72 hours.

(Note: We also covered prophecies that are covered in the question: *"Is the Bible True?"* If someone says it will happen, and it happens, than that was true prophecy.)

(AQ) *DO you believe these prophecies are true or a lie? If a lie, where is your evidence?*

THE EVIDENCE OF THE EMPTY TOMB

The Size

The first thing facing the tomb was the very large stone. According to ancient writings, this stone weighed up to two tons. Once sealed, it would have been almost impossible to remove.

The Seal

The seal of Caesar was attached to the tomb. If any person broke that seal, all of the authority of the Roman Empire would descend upon them and their family. The fear of Rome would have prevented anyone from breaking that seal.

The Soldiers

The Roman security guard consists of sixteen combat-trained soldiers. These men had trained to attack or defend six feet of ground, and they were experts. On the night watch, four men would guard the tomb, while the other twelve slept.

These twelve men would have slept with their backs to the tomb, facing outward. If attacked, they could rise up and confront their enemy. They would be in the way of anyone trying to steal the body.

These precautions proved one thing: No ordinary person could have stolen the body of Jesus.

(AQ) *Do you disagree with this information? If "Yes" – What is wrong with this information? Where is your evidence?*

THE TOMB—OCCUPIED

If you don't believe in the resurrection, I can name only five possibilities to explain the empty tomb. They are:

1. *Unknown Tomb*
2. *Wrong Tomb*—the disciples mistakenly went to a different tomb that was empty.
3. *Legend*
4. *Spiritual*
5. *Hallucination*

(AQ) *Can you think of any other possibilities? If you can, show your evidence.*

The first two examples can be destroyed by the enemies of Jesus. The disciples may have been wrong about the tomb, but Jesus' enemies placed the Roman soldiers to guard the tomb. They *knew* where Jesus was buried. All they had to do was to produce the body. They could not.

The other three possibilities also fail because of the five hundred eyewitnesses recorded in 1 Corinthians 15:6: *"After that He appeared to more than five hundred brethren at one time, most of whom remain until now, but some have fallen asleep."*

The odds are, at that time, most of the 500 will die for their belief.

THE TOMB—EMPTY

So if you accept that the tomb of Jesus was empty, how do you explain it? Again, five possibilities:

1. *Stolen by the Disciples*
2. *Stolen by the Temple Authorities*
3. *The "Swoon Theory"*
4. *The "Passover Plot"*
5. *Jesus Rose from the Dead*

(AQ) *Can you think of another theory? If you can, where is your evidence?*

Stolen by the Disciples

Could the disciples have stolen Jesus' body to create a myth that He had risen from the dead? They were in fear of the Roman government. They thought they would be next.

This is why they had their doors locked when Jesus appeared to them.

(AQ) *Would the disciples, after running away, face the Roman combat-ready guards, to steal the body? Would you lay down your life and die for what you knew to be a lie?*

Stolen by the Temple Authorities

What would be their motive? First of all, they got Pilate to set up the guard at the Tomb in the first place. And even if they could move the stone, they would not have broken the Seal of Rome. They knew the consequences. Second, they would have had to convince the Roman guard to leave their post. For a Roman guard to go AWOL while protecting the Seal of Caesar would have meant a certain painful death *AND* their families.

(AQ) *Why would Roman soldiers go AWOL?*

Consider This: The Resurrection story started in Jerusalem, the place of the crucifixion, and not from the outskirts (Britain) of the Roman Empire.

If the Resurrection was a hoax, the Jewish and Roman authorities needed only produce the body. The Messianic movement would have died at that moment. They did not produce the body because they could not. All Jews, Messianic and otherwise, believed that the tomb was empty.

(AQ) *If you state that the Resurrection is a hoax, where is your evidence? Can you prove it was not?*

The "Swoon Theory"

In 1828, H.E.G. Paulus popularized a theory that Jesus did not actually die on the cross. Supposedly when the soldier thrust the spear into the body, he only pierced a vein and missed the heart.

When your starting point is wrong, you cannot end up in the correct position. Here is the problem with that understanding. At the time of Paulus, medical doctors believed that "bleeding" someone could help them recover faster. So Paulus believed that the loss of blood helped revive Jesus. Thus when Jesus appeared to several of His disciples, they assumed that he rose from the dead. After forty days, Jesus died from His wounds, and nobody ever found His body.

Nineteenth-century rationalists largely accepted this theory because they deliberately sought a reason not to believe in the Resurrection.

(AQ) *Does this theory match the historical facts? Where is your evidence?*

Consider this: A spear was thrust into Jesus' side to confirm He was dead. Blood and water poured out. This separation is one of the surest medical evidence of death.

The Roman soldiers would have suffered the same fate as Jesus if they released Him while still alive. Yet they were so sure that they did not break His legs. Only after Pilate received an official death report would he release the body. Jesus was graveyard dead.

(AG) Only with a great deal of faith can you believe in this theory, but if you do, please answer these questions: *How can a half-dead man, beaten beyond recognition, convince others that He had risen from the dead? How can a beaten man in need of medical attention trick a trained Roman execution squad, escape from heavy wrappings, move a two-ton stone, overcome the soldiers at the tomb, walk fourteen miles to Emmaus, and then convince His disciples He was the conqueror of death? How can a dying man, too weak to carry his cross, inspire the disciples to boldness and courage in the face of death? Where is your evidence?*

Resuscitation would have weakened the faith of His disciples, yet, in the fear of death, their faith remained strong.

The "Passover Plot"

Hugh Schonfield's 1965 book *The Passover Plot* and the 1976 movie based thereon theorized that Jesus arranged His life to fulfill many of the Messianic prophecies.

By means of a drug, he fakes his death on the cross. His fellow conspirator, Joseph of Arimathea, was to take Jesus' body to a tomb for later revival. Then a Roman soldier thrust a spear into Jesus' side, killing him and ruining the plot.

Later, an unknown man is mistaken for Jesus on several occasions. This makes the disciples believe that Jesus has risen from the dead.

This is a modern version of the *"Swoon Theory"* that fails against the historical facts.

(AQ) *If Judas was part of the Passover Plot, why would he try to return the money and hang himself before the death of Jesus? James the Just was Jesus' half-brother, fully convinced that Jesus was risen. Was he unable to recognize his brother? How would you explain the conversion of Paul? Again, with all of the hindrances at the tomb, how did they remove the body? Where is your evidence to substantiate it?*

Jesus rose from the dead.

(AQ) *If this did not happen, explain to me the empty tomb. Can you think of another reason?*

THE EVIDENCE FROM EYEWITNESSES

As mentioned previously, 1 Corinthians 15:6 reports that over five hundred people saw the resurrected Messiah. That works out to over fifty hours of testimony, allowing six minutes for each person. Later, many of them would pay with their lives because of their testimony.

(AQ) *Would you die for what you knew to be a lie?*

You must also consider the character of the witnesses. They weren't all repeating some concocted script. Some, like Thomas and Jacob (James), Jesus' half-brother, were initially unconvinced. They would later die for their testimony.

Some were hostile, like Saul, who would later become Paul. As Saul, he killed the followers of Jesus. After meeting the resurrected Messiah, though, he changed his name, his character, his relationship with God and men, his message, and his mission.

Four times, he suffered the 39 stripes of the whip—not to mention imprisonment, two years of house arrest while chained to a Roman guard, shipwreck, and finally death—all because of his testimony.

(AQ) *Why would he go through this if the Resurrection were a hoax?*

Consider this: A woman saw Him first. You wouldn't record this if you wanted to create a Resurrection hoax.

Why? In that society, a woman was not a legal witness. Even the disciples reject her testimony immediately. This is why Peter and John checked it out themselves. They became the two witnesses required by the Torah.

One final point: *Why was the burial cloth folded? In John 20:6-8 reads "Simon Peter arrived after him and went into the tomb. He saw the strips of linen lying there. He also saw the cloth that had been on Jesus' head. It wasn't lying with the strips of linen but was rolled up separately. Then the other disciple* (John), *who arrived at the tomb first, went inside. He saw and believed."*

In order to understand the significance of the folded napkin, you have to understand a little bit about Hebrew tradition of that day. The folded napkin had to do with the Master and Servant, and every Jewish boy knew this tradition.

When the servant set the dinner table for the master, he made sure that it was exactly the way the master wanted it.

The table was furnished perfectly, and then the servant would wait, just out of sight, until the master had finished eating, and the servant would not dare touch that table, until the master was finished. Now, if the master were done eating, he would rise from the table, wipe his fingers, his mouth, and clean his beard, and would wad up that napkin and toss it onto the table.

The servant would then know to clear the table. In those days, the wadded napkin meant, *'I'm done'*.

But if the master got up from the table, and folded his napkin, and laid it beside his plate, the servant would not dare touch the table, because…the folded napkin meant, **'I'm coming back!'**

THE EVIDENCE OF THE TRANSFORMATION OF THE DISCIPLES

The disciples went from fearing the Jewish authorities and the Roman government to boldly facing them, knowing what could happen. A person will not die for a concoction. They will die for a conviction.

Death of the Early Believers

Matthew: killed with a weapon that had a blade and spike in 60 CE in Ethiopia

Mark: dragged by horses through the streets in Alexandria, Egypt

Luke: hanged on an olive tree in Greece

John: boiled in oil but survived; only apostle to die peacefully.

Peter: crucified upside down on an x-shaped cross

James the Just: thrown over a hundred feet down at the pinnacle of the Temple, then beaten to death with a fuller's club

James the Greater: beheaded at Jerusalem in 44 CE

Bartholomew (Nathanael): flayed to death by a whip and crucified head down

Andrew: whipped severely by seven soldiers, then crucified in Edessa

Thomas: stabbed with a spear in India

Jude (brother of Jesus): killed with arrows

Jude (Jude Thaddeus): crucified in 72 CE in Edessa.

Matthias: stoned and then beheaded in Jerusalem

Barnabas: stoned to death at Salonica

Paul: beheaded by the evil Emperor Nero

Simon the Zealot: crucified

Philip of Bethsaida: crucified

(AQ) *Again, I ask the question: Would you die <u>in this manner</u> if you KNEW you were teaching a lie?*

THE EVIDENCE OF JESUS BEING WORSHIPED AS GOD

The first person to worship Jesus as God was Thomas

Then He said to Thomas, *"Reach here with your finger, and see My hands; and reach here your hand and put it into My side; and do not be unbelieving, but believing." Thomas answered and said to Him, "My Lord and my God!" Jesus said to him, Because you have seen Me, have you believed? Blessed are they who did not see, and yet believed"* John 20:27-29.

Thomas will die for this belief. *Will you?*

THE EVIDENCE OF THE CHURCH

What established the Church? Without the Resurrection, this would have never have happened. It changed twelve cowards into men willing to die for this belief. These twelve men turned the Roman Empire upside down.

No delusion could have produced this. Luke wrote in Acts 4:33, *"with great power the Apostles gave witness to the resurrection of Lord Jesus."*

Did the mere teachings of Jesus form the corner piece of this movement? **No.** The heart of this worship was the fact that a crucified Messiah was now alive.

THE ORDER OF THE RESURRECTION

"But now the Messiah has been raised from the dead, the <u>*first fruits*</u> *of those who are asleep. For since by a man came death, by a man also came the resurrection of the dead. For as in Adam all die, so also in the Messiah all will be made alive. But each in his own order:* <u>Messiah the first fruits</u>, *after that* <u>those who are the Messiah's at His coming</u>, *then comes the end, when He hands*

over the kingdom to the God and Father, when He has abolished all rule and all authority and power" 1 Corinthians 15:20-24 NASB.

Look at the order:

1) The Messiah the First Fruits

2) Those who are the Messiah's at His coming

3) The end

(Side Question: *Where, in that order, is the Pre or Mid-Tribulation Rapture?*)

SUMMARY

When I accepted the Resurrection of Jesus on Easter Sunday in 1979, I immediately entered the next battleground, and like the eagle with the snake, redefined it. Prepare yourselves and join me for *"Is Jesus God?"*

IS JESUS GOD?

(AG) Questions you ask the Atheist to make him think.

Jesus made a claim that is unique among the founders of the major religions. Consider:

- Buddha
- Confucius
- Mohammed

None of them claimed to be God. To ignore Jesus' claim is to reject Him. If Jesus is God, His message of redemption is the most important message ever.

Is Jesus our Creator God? The Bible affirms in several places that Jesus the Messiah is the Creator God. For example, *"In the beginning was the* <u>Word</u>, *and the* <u>Word</u> *was with God, and the* <u>Word</u> *was God"* (John 1:1).

The *"Word"*, in Greek, is *Logos*. In Aramaic, which was the language Jesus spoke, it is *Memra*. It means a divine individual. The context says that it's Jesus the Messiah (John 1:1, 3), and *"For by him* (Jesus the Messiah) *were all things created"* (Colossians 1:16).

If this is true, we should expect to see the parallelism between what happened at Creation and the works of Jesus during His ministry on earth. *What do we find?*

FOUR EVIDENCES

Before we start, let's consider what kind of evidence we need. Four of the essential and distinctive elements of Creation, as revealed in Genesis 1 and elsewhere in the Bible, are:

1. **Creation out of nothing and/or existing materials.** Creation involved the act of God producing immediately and instantaneously matter not previously existent. For example, the Creation of the heavens and the earth as recorded in Genesis 1:1. Creation also involved the shaping, combining, or transforming of existing materials. An example was when God created Adam from the dust of the ground (Genesis 2:7). He also created Eve from Adam's rib (Genesis 2:21-22).

2. **The Giving of Life**. Creation involved the imparting of life to previously lifeless matter.

3. **The Methods God used**. The mechanism of Creation was the Word of the Lord. *What does that*

mean? It means what God said it should happen …and it happened.

4. **The purpose or motive of God in creating.** God created in order to display His glory, to make known His power, His wisdom, His will, and His holy name. He also desired to receive glory from His created beings.

We should not expect to find EXACT parallels between the miracles of Jesus and what happened at Creation. *Why?* Jesus did not come to re-create the universe, but *"to seek and to save that which was lost,"* and *"to give his life a ransom for many."* With this in mind, let us compare these four aspects of creation with the works of Jesus.

1. Creation out of nothing and / or existing materials.

Several of Jesus' miracles involved the creation of new material. Jesus' first miraculous sign to His disciples involved the creation of wine. The water had been turned into wine. This required the instantaneous creation of the molecules that made up the wine: grape sugar, carbon dioxide, coloring matter, etc.

Other examples include the two times when Jesus fed a multitude. He fed more than five thousand people from five loaves and two fish and also fed more than four thousand people from seven loaves and a few little fish. Both times, some bread and fish were preexisting. Jesus either caused these original items to multiply or created new loaves and fishes until everyone was fed.

Either way, Jesus created extra bread and fish to feed many thousands of people, but also provided many baskets full of leftovers.

This miracle involved the creation of the appropriate food molecules and their immediate arrangement into the complex structures of baked bread and cooked fish.

Jesus' healing miracles (including lepers, paralytics, and the blind) involved the instant repair of body tissues and the instantaneous growth or regrowth of healthy cells. This created healthy, working body parts to replace the diseased, non-functioning parts.

(AQ) *If Jesus is not God, what would be the process you would use to produce these results? Show your evidence.*

2. The giving of life.

Jesus gave life to the dead on three occasions: to a widow's son, to Jairus' daughter, and to his friend Lazarus. The first two had died recently; in medical terms, they had "flat-lined" for an hour or more, and Jesus called for the immediate restarting their stopped heartbeats and other biological processes.

In the case of Lazarus, Martha tells us, "...*by this time there is a bad odour, for he has been there (in the grave) four days*" (John 11:39). This proves the process of decomposition, whereby a dead body becomes dust, had already started. Jesus called Lazarus back to life, and his decaying molecules became, again, a living human being.

We have a parallel with the sixth day of creation, when God formed Adam from the dust of the ground and breathed into his nostrils the breath of life. Adam became a "speaking spirit." Likewise by the words of Jesus, three people received, again, a "speaking spirit."

(AQ) *If Jesus is not God, how would you, as a human being, raise the dead?*

3. The methods God used.

Jesus used a variety of means in performing His miracles. These included touching lepers, the blind and the deaf; the use of saliva to heal a deaf-mute and a blind man; the use of clay (with instructions to wash) to heal a blind man; and the word of command to heal, to raise the dead, and to drive out demons.

What happened in all these cases? Jesus willed the event to happen, and it did. The best illustration is the healing of the nobleman's son. Jesus was at Cana in Galilee, and a royal official asked Him to travel to Capernaum to heal his son, who was close to death (John 4:46-53). Rather than travel, Jesus willed the sick boy to recover. Capernaum was about 17 miles from Cana, much too far for the sick son, or anyone else in Capernaum, to hear Jesus feel any influence from His physical presence in Cana. Yet the boy recovered, and at the very moment Jesus spoke.

Jesus willed the water to become wine and it did. He willed the bread and fish to create itself and they did. He willed the ten lepers to become well. After they left Him to see the priests, they were healed.

Consider this: a Gentile centurion, recognizing Jesus' authority, sent servants requesting healing for his servant (Luke 7:6-10). He knew the voice of Jesus would be effective. What was the result? The servant healed.

(AQ) *If Jesus is not God, how would you, as a human being, perform these miracles?*

4. The purpose or motive of God in creating.

The miracles would show Jesus' glory. After Jesus' first miraculous sign to His disciples—turning water into wine—

John says He *"manifested forth his glory; and his disciples believed on him."*

When Jesus heard that Lazarus was sick He said, *"This sickness is not unto death, but for the glory of God, that the Son of God might be glorified."* After Lazarus had died and before Jesus raised him to life, He said to Martha, *"Said I not unto you, that, if you would believe, you should see the glory of God?"*

John calls Jesus' miracles, signs and shows which way the signs point: *"these are written, that you might believe that Jesus is the Messiah, the Son of God; and that believing you might have life through his name."*

Jesus the Messiah is the Creator God. During His earthly life and ministry He did the very things we would expect the Creator God to do and did them in the way that we would expect—by His word of authority and the exercise of His will.

(AQ) *If Jesus is not God, what process would you use to produce these results?*

JESUS AND SALVATION.

Jesus also claimed that His way of salvation is the only way mankind can return to a right relationship with a holy God. We can be prove this through the following:

1) The Evidence of History;

2) The Evidence of the Impact of History;

3) The Evidence of Messianic Prophecy;

4) The Evidence of Miracles;

5) The Evidence of the Virgin Birth;

6) The Evidence of Divine Attributes;

7) The Evidence of the Argument: liar, lunatic, legend or Lord.

Let's study each of these:

THE EVIDENCE OF HISTORY

Skeptics have questions whether Jesus ever existed. These claims are never made by knowledgeable historians never make such claims.

Those who try to dismiss the Messiah as a myth do not use historical evidence. The following chart represents a partial list of non-believing sources that give evidence to the life of the Messiah.

Early Non-Believing References to Jesus

WRITER	DATE	WRITING	RELEVANCE
Thallus	52ce	Chronicle	Solar eclipse at the crucifixion
Josephus	93ce	Antiquities	References John the Baptist, Jesus, and James the Just
Pliny the Younger	112ce	Letter to Trajan	Information about early believers of Messiah
Cornelius Tacitus	116ce	Annals	Information on the origin and spread of body of Messiah
Serenius Granianus	115-38ce	Letter to Hadrian	Discusses charges brought against the body of Messiah
Suetonius	120ce	Life of Nero	Reports punishment inflicted on the body of Messiah
Phlegon	140ce	Olympiads	Solar eclipse at the crucifixion
Lucian of Somosata	170ce	The Death of Perefrine	Hostile testimony about early body of Messiah

Many rabbis have references that discuss the life of Jesus. Not one of them question whether Jesus existed. Even present-day historians will not deny the history of Jesus the Messiah.

THE EVIDENCE OF THE IMPACT OF HISTORY

Here are similarities between the lives of Socrates and Jesus:

- Both tried to improve mankind;
- Both gathered disciples;
- Both unjustly died.

Socrates left his world unchanged with his teachings all but forgotten. When Jesus died, He forever changed mankind. **WHY?** Socrates was a man, but Jesus was the God-Man.

History has never been the same since the coming of Jesus. It divided history itself into two ages—B.C. (Before Christ) and A.D. (Anno Domini or "Year of our Lord"). These days, we see those secularized as BCE/CE (Before Common Era/Common Era), but the same dividing point exists. Although off by a few years thanks to a medieval monk's miscalculation, the "Common Era" starts with the birth of Jesus.

The New Testament gives very few details on His life, focusing on his three-year ministry. From this brief period sprang the largest religious following in history. His recorded deeds and teachings represent truth to countless millions of people. His impact is clear through His claim that He is God.

(AQ) *If the Messiah does not exist, can you explain the division of history between B.C. and A.D.? How?*

THE EVIDENCE OF MESSIANIC PROPHECY

Consider this: Jesus is one of over forty Jewish men who claimed to be the Messiah. This forces a question: *How do we know that Jesus is really the promised Messiah?*

These facts come from Messianic prophecies. Because of the volume and nature of these prophecies, the laws of probability forbid that anyone could fulfill them all by accident. Written four hundred years or more before the Messiah was born, the prophecies recorded many specific details so that He could be identified when He came.

What if Jesus manipulated his life to try to become the Messiah? This is impossible. Jesus' enemies fulfilled many of the prophecies by their own actions. He could not have faked the accounts of Jesus' suffering, not to mention His resurrection from the dead.

Even before the birth of Jesus, the Jews had carefully constructed the Old Testament prophecy lists concerning the Messiah. These lists were among the discoveries at Qumran in 1948.

Jesus based His entire ministry on the fact that He was the promised Messiah. He taught His disciples that the prophecies about Him must be fulfilled, and the entire Old Testament spoke of Him. Paul's teaching that Jesus was the Messiah is the key to understanding the Old Testament (2 Corinthians 3:14-17). Jesus claiming He was the Messiah led to His crucifixion.

If Jesus did not fulfill all of the Messianic prophecies, then the entire New Testament is a lie. No other religion has had such a test imposed upon it.

Jesus has already fulfilled 454 identifiable prophecies as the "suffering servant," known in Jewish terms as *"Messiah Ben Joseph."* When He returns as "King of Kings," known in Jewish terms as *"Messiah Ben David,"* He will fulfill the rest of the Messianic prophecies.

Jesus could not have been an impostor who carefully arranged the fulfillment of all the Messianic prophecies without supernatural assistance. To reject Jesus as the Messiah defies the laws of probability.

(AQ) *If Jesus is not the Messiah, can you name any person in history that was able to fulfill the 454 Messianic prophecies, twenty in one day?*

THE EVIDENCE OF MIRACLES

We have looked at the miracles of Jesus and understood that a normal human being does not have that power. Let us now consider the concept of miracles through science.

A person can claim to be God, but then he must prove it. A claim to deity requires extraordinary evidence. Jesus provided it by miracles. Miracles that occur in the Bible are a means of authenticating divine revelation.

When Jesus began His ministry, He unleashed a series of miracles that caught the world's attention. He healed the sick, gave sight to the blind, fed thousands of people from a handful of food, demonstrated power over nature, and even raised the dead. These miracles served to validate his claims (Acts 2:22). Jesus told his listeners that if they didn't believe his words, they should believe his works (John 10:37–38).

His enemies never questioned that the miracles happened. The Pharisees met, not to decide whether or not Jesus performed miracles, but to plan how they could stop Him from doing more. They told everyone that he performed miracles by the power of Satan (Mark 3:22).

Major point: the enemies of Jesus never tried to expose him as a clever magician or publicly explain how He was able to do His magic tricks.

For many unbelievers, the miracles are obstacles. Today, too many people will reject that which defies scientific explanation. Many theologians accept Jesus as divine but reject the miraculous stories about Him. This has a major problem. It's inconsistent with the eyewitness testimony. Any portrayal of Jesus other than the miraculous Messiah is a myth. *What does that mean?*

To deny that Jesus performed any miracles is to deny that Jesus is divine. The discrediting of miracles comes from an atheist bias — everything must have naturalistic explanations because God does not exist. This should not be an issue for a believer. If God exists, then miracles are possible. The question is not, "Can miracles occur?" but, *"Have miracles occurred?"*

Miracles by definition defy science — or more correctly, *operational* science. This is science that you can demonstrate yourself in everyday life or lab conditions. But the principles of *origins science* are consistent with certain miracles in the past.

Origins science uses the principles of causality (everything that has a beginning has a cause) and analogy (e.g., we observe that only intelligence can generate complex coded information in the present, so we can reasonably assume the same for the past) to conclude that life — not to mention the universe itself — is a miracle by an intelligent Creator God.

If miracles have occurred as the direct intervention of God, then God may alter outcomes on His whim. Such as:

First, Miracles are an *addition* to natural laws rather than an exception. Natural laws require isolated systems. For example, Newton's First Law of Motion says *"objects will continue in a straight line at constant speed — if no unbalanced force is acting."* So you can defy that law when an unbalanced force acts. That's a good thing; otherwise, nothing could ever change direction!

Suppose an atheist claims Jesus couldn't have walked on water because it would violate Archimedes' Principle: *"Objects will sink in water if they weigh more than the buoyant force."* But this is true only if no other forces are operating. For example, if you were dangling from a helicopter, you wouldn't sink. Archimedes' Principle can't prevent other forces from acting.

If God exists, no system is truly isolated. *What does that mean?* You cannot disallow miracles unless you can prove God doesn't exist. If Jesus really were God Incarnate, He could certainly bring other forces into play without violating science.

(AQ) *Can you, by applying Newton's first Law of motion, prove miracles cannot exist? If so, how? Produce your evidence.*

Second, scientific laws are *descriptive* of what we observe happening regularly. An example would be a map of a coastline. If you treated scientific laws as unbending, (i.e. the cause of the observed consistencies), you would claim that the drawing of the map is the cause of the coastline's shape.

Believers don't advocate just any *'god'* who may or may not be changeable. They identify the Designer with the faithful God of the Bible—YHVH, the God of Abraham, Isaac and Jacob.

The Bible explains that:

- We are made in the image of a rational God (Genesis 1:26-27),

- God is a God of order not of confusion (1 Corinthians 14:33),

- God gave man dominion over Creation, (Genesis 1:28), and

- He commanded honesty (Exodus 20:16).

Applying this concept within a correct understanding of scientific laws, we get a worldview that historically led to science without discarding miracles.

The founders of modern science, like modern creationists, regarded *natural laws* as descriptions of the way God upholds His creation in a regular and repeatable way (Colossians 1:15-17). The miracles are God's way of upholding His creation in a special way for special reasons.

Because the creation finished at the end of day six (Genesis 2:1-3), creationists following the Bible would expect that God has since worked through natural laws except where He has revealed miracles in the scriptures.

Since natural laws are descriptive, they cannot specify what cannot happen. *What does that mean?* They cannot rule out miracles. Scientific laws do not cause or forbid anything anymore than a crooked line on a map causes the coastline.

Creationists seek natural laws for every aspect of operational science apart from Creation itself. They would not invoke a miracle to explain any repeating event in nature *in the present.*

If you believe atoms hold together by miraculous means, consider this concept: *"Natural laws"* help us make predictions about future events. In the case of the atom, the electrons stay in their orbitals by the positive electric charge and large mass of the nucleus.

For example, this enables us to make predictions about how strongly a particular electron is held by a particular atom, making the study of chemistry possible. This is an example of Colossians 1:17. Simply saying *"God upholds the electron,"* doesn't help us make predictions.

> *There are people who will say, "If we allowed appealing to God anytime we don't understand something, then science itself would be impossible, for science proceeds on the assumption of natural causality." This argument is a red herring. It's true that science is not compatible with just any form of theism, particularly a theism that holds to a capricious god who intervenes so often that the contrast between primary and secondary causality is unintelligible. But Christian theism holds that secondary causality is God's usual mode and primary causality is infrequent. That is why Christianity, far from hindering the development of science, actually provided the womb for its birth and development."* (Christianity and the Nature of Science: A Philosophical Investigation, Baker Book House Company, Grand Rapids, Michigan, page 226, 1989.)

Any evidence for or against God's existence–a book, a fossil, a supposed miracle—may just be His intervention, perhaps hidden from our understanding. Suppose God will cheat or boast that He can or does intervene in our lives and the natural order to create a species, for prayer, for adulation, or any purpose not even disclosed to us. Then observation of the world, from the affairs of the tiniest microbes to galactic catastrophe, is all futile. *Why?* They are all at the whim of a fickle god who will deceive us when it suits him.

Therefore to test that God exists by appeal to observations in and of this world and its affairs is futile. If God has intervened in the world even once, then no observation or consequential conjecture we can make is reliable.

Somehow, an extraordinary idea has arisen that the disbelievers in miracles consider them coldly and fairly, while the believers accept them only in connection with dogma. This reverse is actually true.

The believers accept miracles (rightly or wrongly) because they have evidence. The unbelievers deny miracles (rightly or wrongly) because of doctrine.

C. S. Lewis pointed out that arguing against miracles based on the alleged total uniformity of nature is circular reasoning (from *Miracles*):

> *"If circular reasoning is absolutely 'uniform experience' against miracles, meaning they never happened, then they never have. Unfortunately, we know the experience against them to be uniform only if we know that all the reports of them are false. We know all the reports are false*

only if we know already that miracles have never occurred. In fact, we are arguing in a circle."

Let us suppose that a clever person makes an observation that purports to prove a miracle has occurred, showing God has intervened just once. We cannot thereafter trust our observation on any other point. *Why?*

It may be another intervention. Since the tool science is ideally rigorous observation and conjecture, the miracle would seem to discredit that very tool as a way to discover the nature of the world. Since observation, by this test, becomes a discredited tool, its proof that a miracle has occurred is also discredited.

Actually, the exact opposite is true. Without a belief that the universe was made by a God of order and that we are made in the image of this God, we have no basis for either an orderly universe or that the trustworthiness of our own thoughts.

As an atheist, I could not prove the universe is orderly. *Why?* Because my only proofs would be the order I was trying to prove.

Atheists can treat these premises as axioms — accepted as true without proof. For believers, they are formulas since they follow from the concepts of Scripture. Similarly, an atheist can't prove that their thoughts are rational because the proofs would have to assume this very rationality. Yet evolution would select only for survival advantage, not rationality.

Either God exists, and He cheats with miracles, or the world obeys strict rules of action and consequence.

If the former, we can prove nothing, even by the most rigorous observation and conjecture. *Why?* Most philosophers of science agree you cannot *prove* things with science. Scientific progress comes from *disproving* things. This becomes very clear when you understand the underlying logic.

If the latter, our world is true to its appearance and we have a chance of understanding it. You cannot derive an orderly universe from the proposition *God does not exist*. You need to accept an orderly universe as a *brute fact*. This, ironically, was plagiarized from the believer's world view.

We have set up a *false dilemma*. However, an alternative, as explained, is a God of order who used miracles for Creation, and in rare occasions at other times when working out His program. But it normally works by what we call *natural law*. The logical feasibility has ample proof in practice from the good science discovered by miracle believers.

(AQ) *If God does not exist, how do you explain the order of 'natural laws' in the universe? What is your evidence? Where did you get your facts?*

THE EVIDENCE OF THE VIRGIN BIRTH

God, through Moses, wrote in Genesis 3:15, *"And I will put enmity between thee and the woman, and between thy seed and* her seed; *it shall bruise thy head, and thou shalt bruise his heel."*

Point: Man carries the seed, not the woman, yet it says, *"her seed."*

Seven hundred years before Jesus was born, Isaiah prophesied in Isaiah 7:14 *"Therefore the Lord himself shall give you a sign; Behold,* a virgin *(Almah) shall conceive and bear a son, and shall call his name Immanuel."*

Both Matthew and Luke provide detailed accounts of the virgin birth to show its fulfillment. For Jesus to be the Messiah, this had to happen.

Two Hebrew words can mean virgin--*Almah* and *Bethulah*. The word *"almah,"* used in Isaiah 7:14, means a young woman of marriageable age. Isaiah, through the Holy Spirit, used this word, not *bethulah*. He had to combine both ideas (virgin and marriageable age) into one word to meet the historical situation and the prophetic concept.

The word *virgin* in Greek is *parthenos*, which means a virgin, marriageable maiden or young married woman, pure virgin. When the Jewish translators of the Septuagint, completed around 280-246 BCE in Alexandria, translated Isaiah 7:14 into Greek, they used *parthenos*. To them, the verse meant that the Messiah would be born of a virgin.

Many people deny the virgin birth on the grounds that it's biologically impossible. That <u>IS THE WHOLE POINT! It IS impossible</u>! That is what makes the virgin birth a sign. If it were not a miracle, it would not be a *sign*.

Would you sooner believe God became a man by the natural reproductive process of humans rather than supernaturally? All of this point to the fact that the Bible is true.

The Jewish nation is also a *miracle* and a *sign*. Sarah miraculously conceived in her old age, and Isaac became the sign of the start of the Jewish nation.

C. S. Lewis applied scientific concepts to the virginal conception of the Messiah: the zygote arose from the Holy Spirit's action on Mary's ovaries, i.e. an *addition* to her system. (God may have even used Joseph's DNA since Jesus needed to be a descendant of David.) But after that, the embryo developed in the normal manner.

(AQ) *If a miracle of birth cannot happen, can you give a different explanation how the Jewish nation exists without the miracle of Isaac's birth? Where is your evidence?*

THE EVIDENCE OF DIVINE ATTIBUTES

Jesus was not just an extraordinary human being, he is God. The deity of the Messiah is explicit in the Scriptures. The writers of the New Testament, at many times, directly referred to Jesus as God (Titus 2:13; John 14:9; Romans 9:5; John 1:1; John 20:28).

Jesus' enemies also understood that He claimed to be God. *How do we know this?* They accused Him of blasphemy (John 10:33).

Jesus' claim has compelling, strong evidence. Jesus possesses all the attributes of God even though he took the form of a human body. Colossians 2:9 says, *"for in Him dwells all the fullness of the Godhead bodily."*

Consider the attributes of Jesus in the following chart:

Jesus' Attributes to Deity

Characteristic	Scripture
Preexistence	John 8:58
Creator of the Universe	Hebrews 1:2
Sinless	II Corinthians 5:21
Forgives Sins	Mark 2:5
Power over Nature	Mark 4:41
Raise the Dead	John 11:1-44
Power over Disease	John 9:25-32
Resurrection	I Corinthians 15:3-5
Eternal	Revelation 1:8; Revelation 22:13
Holy	John 6:69
Omnipresent	Matthew 28:20
Omnipotent	Matthew 28:18
Immutable	Hebrews 13:8
Sustainer of Creation	Hebrews 1:3; Colossians 1:17
Brings Salvation	I John 4:14
Accepts Worship	John 9:38
Object of Prayer	Acts 7:59
Universal Judge	Matthew 25:31-46
Omniscient	John 16:30

No other religious leader has ever demonstrated such powerful attributes in his life. Also, no other religious leader substantiated the claim to be God. In John 14:9, Jesus told His disciples that those who have seen Him have seen God.

The message of the Bible centers on the truth that a right relationship with God only comes from a relationship with Jesus the Messiah (John 14:6). *What does that mean?* When a person believes in Jesus, he/she is believing in God (John 12:44).

(AQ) *Can you name any other human being who processes these attributes? Where is your evidence?*

THE EVIDENCE OF THE ARGUMENT: LIAR, LUNATIC, LEGEND, OR LORD

Jesus claimed to be God a number of times. You have two alternatives: It could be true or false. If you reject His claim, again, you have two alternatives.

The *first* alternative is that Jesus knew it was false, making Him a **liar**. Then He was also a hypocrite, saying one thing and doing another. Furthermore He had a demon because he misled people against the word of God. Last, He was a fool. *Why?* He died on the cross because of His claim to be God.

The *second* alternative is that Jesus DIDN'T know His claim was false. He was sincere but self-deceived, making Him sincerely deluded and a **lunatic**. His teachings and actions do not back up this alternative. The life of the Messiah has no evidence of the abnormality and imbalance found in a deranged person.

Some choose a *third* alternative, that the divine claims of Jesus are a **legend**. He never did miracles or claimed to be God; His followers in the third and fourth centuries added those things. If He were to return today, he would immediately reject the Bible account.

Here is the problem with that theory. We have already established that the four biographies (Gospels) of Jesus first appeared within the lifetime of the people who had actually met Him—certainly no later than 70 CE.

Could a legend have gained such circulation and impact in the form of the four Gospels?

It strains belief. This would be like someone in our own time writing a biography of John F. Kennedy and saying he claimed to be God, forgave people's sins, and rose from the dead. Nobody would accept this as true. *Why?* Too many people alive today still remember Kennedy.

The legend theory does not work because of the early date of the gospel manuscripts.

(AQ) *If you believe it's a legend, where are your sources?*

The Vatican, holder of the original documents, would like to know.

By the process of elimination, we come to the *fourth* alternative: His claims are true. Jesus is **LORD**.

SUMMARY: THE BRAZEN SERPENT

John 3:14-15 says that life begins with looking to the Son of Man: *"Just as Moses lifted up the serpent in the desert, so must the Son of Man be lifted up; so that everyone who trusts in him may have eternal life."*

Before Moses lifted up the brazen serpent, people died. Afterward (Numbers 21:4-9), people lived. The children of Israel had to know three things to prevent death. They needed to know the snake bit them, that they had a God-given remedy against death, and that the remedy was not good until applied.

You must apply these same three processes to Jesus for you to have eternal life. You must know that sin has bitten you, that God has provided a remedy against eternal death, and that you must apply the remedy to receive God's healing. The remedy comes from Jesus.

One man in Scripture understood this substitution process: *Barabbas. Why?*

1. He knew he was a justly condemned sinner.
2. He knew Jesus was an innocent sufferer.
3. He knew the innocent sufferer has taken his place.
4. He knew he had done nothing to merit that substitution.
5. He also knew that Jesus' substitution in his place satisfied the law.

(AQ) *Do you have the same knowledge as Barabbas?*

You have three choices:

1. You do not believe in the Resurrection.

2. You are not ready to choose, but this is effectively the first choice.

3. You do believe in the Resurrection. This choice will change your life. You cannot choose this and not change.

If you are reading this book as an agnostic, do *not* take this choice lightly. Here is why: I, you, and God *will stand by it*. Today, the decision is yours. Thank God and then consider, *"What will you do with Jesus?"* Someday the choice will be His. Then the question will be, *"What will He do with you?"* You can say it with your mouth, but the real vote is in your heart, and God sees it.

John 12:32 says, *"And I, if I be lifted up from the earth, will draw all men unto me."*

(AQ) *What is your Choice?*

As you, the believer, go through this chapter, remember the first point. You need not prove your case to the atheist. The atheist must prove his. When he/she tries, you will find a very strong use for the four "Killer Questions."

The next major battleground looks at other religions. Some do not have a Messiah, and others have a different Messiah. Let's face the first battlefront with *"Is Jesus the only way to God? (Part 1)."*

IS JESUS THE ONLY WAY TO GOD? PART 1

(AQ) Questions you ask the Atheist to make him think)

INTRODUCTION

Jesus came into this world to show the way to live. If you are a Gentile believer, you are part of the *"commonwealth of Israel."*

Picture this: You are in a train station and five lines of people are getting onto trains, one going east and the rest in different directions. Signs above the gates clearly spell out the destinations of these trains. If you get into the wrong line, you cannot blame the railroad for finishing at the wrong destination. Jesus is pointing out the right line to board the right train to the right destination.

TRUTH IS TRUTH

When your doctor finds that you have dangerously high blood pressure, what would the doctor do? He would warn you that unless you change your way of living, you are going to die soon. If you do not pay attention, you are a fool and deserve to die. You cannot blame the doctor. He did not give you extreme hypertension. You did it yourself. *What does that mean?*

Some people argue that while Jesus embodies the truth for some, He may not be the truth for all. The danger in this statement is the implication that all religions are true. In reality, though, "religious truth" and "objective truth" are the same. Likewise with "scientific truth" and "religious truth." Truth is always truth.

Truth always exist outside of your feelings and thoughts. You must discover it. If it's truth, it is truth for all. Two opposing viewpoints cannot be right. Both can be wrong, but both cannot be right.

RELIGIONS ARE NOT EQUAL

Although other religions have elements of truth, they mix with error. If you took a *comparative religions* course in college, you would research for the commonalities within all of them. The result is that you accept the commonality and reject the differences.

But what's the first item you would reject by this process? Most likely, you would eliminate the Messiah. This idea appears only in Christianity, Messianic Judaism and Judaism. These faiths, with their differences, use the same source—the Bible. No other religion uses this source. If Jesus is the Savior only for some people, He lied and thus is the Savior of no one.

Some truths can be relative. "Hot chocolate is good." Is that true? That's a matter of taste. It could be true for you, but not for someone else. If I say, "I really like hot chocolate," that can be objectively true because it only depends on *my* taste.

But what about ideas? Are ideas relative? What if I say, "Jesus is Lord?" Someone else is welcome to disagree, but this is a truth claim. I'm staking out an area of reality and saying this is true.

But what do I mean by 'true'? What corresponds to reality is true. If Jesus is Lord, then He is, no matter how I respond to the claim. I tolerate those with differing beliefs on this point, and they should tolerate my belief. But tolerance does not mean that everyone is right—or that we give up our own truth claims.

TRUTH AND RELIGION

With religion and philosophy, some people do not believe that any one belief is true. They might point out disagreements between all belief systems as proof of the futility of trying to say that any single one is true.

Or sometimes they give analogies, with one of the most popular being the blind men and the elephant. In all variations of the story, the point is that by examining different parts of an elephant, all the blind men concluded it was something different.

One man touched the tail and said it was a rope. Another felt the tusk and thought it was hard and sharp. Yet another felt the ear and said it must be soft and flexible. *"You see,"* says the person offering the example, *"they all grasped parts of the same truth. Similarly, all religions are true in their own way."*

But does this illustration hold up? Is it really the same as our hot chocolate example—a matter of taste?

On closer examination, we learn at least two key problems. **First**, all the men got it wrong! **Second**, knowing just a part of something is not the same as knowing the bigger picture. The men had a truth to grasp—a real, live elephant—but all the men missed out on it.

Now let's take a look at a few religions and philosophies in light of the elephant illustration. Judaism and Christianity believe in only one God, personal and distinctly separate from His creation. Pantheism claims that everything is part of the impersonal divine. Hinduism recognizes potentially thousands of gods. Atheists claim there is no god. *Are these four worldviews really describing different parts of the same thing?*

Since they flatly contradict one another, how could they all describe different aspects of the same thing? After all, God cannot both exist and not exist at the same time. Neither can God be both personal and impersonal, everything and separate from creation at the same time and in the same way. And of course, God can't be both one and thousands.

If we look at the situation rationally, then either all religions and philosophies are wrong or at most one is true. This is not to preclude commonalities between religions and philosophies. But they differ greatly on the big issues such as the nature of God, the human condition, and the way of salvation or spiritual liberation.

Many people contend that all religions provide spiritual guidance and basically the same outcome. Such statements demonstrate insubstantial knowledge of world religions because certainly they all differ. The aforementioned comparative religion studies tend to reduce religion down to a close common denominator that turns out quite different from what the founders intended.

However, something about the Messiah sets it apart from religion. Non-Messianic religions are man's search for

God, but with the Messiah, God is searching for man. All other religions come from sinful man; whereas the Messianic religion's founder is God. Other religions rest on teachings, but the Messianic religions stem from a person.

Jesus' teachings result from who He is. His invitation was not merely to follow His teachings but to follow Him. Jesus did not simply teach about the Resurrection and the way of salvation; He said that He is the Resurrection and the way to God (John 14:6; John 11:25). He is not just another religious leader who spoke to us in a different way; He is God among us showing us the way to everlasting life.

What does that mean? If the God of the Bible is the true God, then all other gods are nonexistent, and nobody should worship them. Contrary to popular religious thought, religion does not evolve upward. A religion erodes downward if it causes man to rejects the revelation of God. Other religions are subjective, but the Messianic religions arises from objective facts. If the claims of the Messiah are true, then other religious leaders can't claim His authority. This makes their teachings, of necessity, false.

MAJOR RELIGION'S BELIEFS ABOUT GOD

We all want to make it through life with success. This brings us to a question. *Do the world religions offer anything that might give our lives greater depth and direction?*

Let's take a look at the following: Hinduism, New Age, Buddhism, and Islam. We are going to give a brief description of each, their view of God, and what a person can gain from them. Each has sects with differing shades of belief, but we are going to focus on core theology.

Hinduism

Most Hindus worship one being of the ultimate oneness through a number of representations of gods and goddesses. These different deities become incarnate within idols, temples, gurus, rivers, animals, etc.

Hindus believe their position in this present life results from *karma* — their good or bad actions in a previous life. Therefore, it provides a possible explanation for suffering and evil in this life. If your previous behavior was evil, you might justifiably experience tremendous hardships in this life. You deserve pain, disease, poverty, or a disaster like a flood because of your own bad karma.

A Hindu's goal is to become free from continuous reincarnations and find rest. Only the soul matters.

Hinduism gives you freedom to choose how to work toward spiritual perfection. This cycle of karma offers three possible ways:

1. Be lovingly devoted to any of the Hindu deities.
2. Grow in knowledge through meditation of oneness. Realize that circumstances in life are not real, selfhood is an illusion, and only oneness is real.
3. Be dedicated to the various religious ceremonies and rites.

New Age

New Age promotes the development of your own power or deity. The deity, of New Age is not a transcendent, personal God who created the universe. It's a higher consciousness within yourself. You would see yourself as deity, the cosmos, and the universe. In fact, everything you see, hear, feel, or imagine becomes deified.

New Age presents itself as a collection of ancient spiritual traditions. It acknowledges many gods and goddesses, just like Hinduism. The earth is a source of all spirituality and has its own intelligence, emotions, and deity. Superseding all of this is self. Self is the originator, controller and power over all. No reality exists outside what you determine.

New Age teaches a wide variety of Eastern mysticism and spiritual, metaphysical, and psychic techniques, such as breathing exercises, chanting, drumming, and meditating. These supposedly develop an altered consciousness in their own divinity.

If you experience anything negative, such as failures, sadness, anger or selfishness, you consider it an illusion. Because you believe yourself completely sovereign over your life, nothing it is wrong, negative or painful. Eventually your mind will develop a spirituality recognizing no objective, external reality. You have at this point become a god, creating your own reality.

Buddhism

Buddhists do not worship any gods or God—not even the Buddha, as non-Buddhists often think. This creates a major problem. The Buddha never claimed to be God or divine. Buddhists say he has obtained what they are also seeking—spiritual enlightenment. This brings freedom from any continuous cycle of life and death.

Most Buddhists believe a person has countless rebirths, which include suffering. As a Buddhist, you seek to end these rebirths. You believe your cravings, aversion and delusion cause these rebirths. Your goal is to purify your heart and to let go of all yearnings toward sensual desires and attachment to yourself.

You would follow a list of religious principles and dedicated meditation. When you meditate, it is not the same as praying or focusing on a God. It is more of a self-discipline. Through practiced meditation, you may reach *nirvana* — the "blowing out" of the flame of desire. Buddhism provides something true of most major religions: disciplines, values, and directives you may want to live by.

Islam

Muslims believe in one Almighty God, named Allah, is infinitely superior to and transcendent from all humankind. As a Muslim, you would view Allah as the creator of the universe and the source of all good and all evil. Everything that happens is Allah's will. He is a powerful and strict judge who will be merciful toward you depending upon the sufficiency of your life's good works and religious devotion. Your relationship with Allah is as a servant to Allah.

Though you would honor several prophets, you consider Mohammed the last prophet, and his words and lifestyle are your authority. (If asked about Jesus, you will grudgingly acknowledge Him as a secondary prophet.)

You must follow five religious duties:

1. Repeat a creed about Allah and Mohammed;

2. Recite certain prayers in Arabic five times a day;

3. Give to the needy;

4. One month each year, fast from food, drink, sex, and smoking from sunrise to sunset;

5. Pilgrimage once in your lifetime to worship at a shrine in Mecca.

At death, based on your faithfulness to these duties, you hope to enter paradise with their 72 virgins. If not, you will receive eternal punishment in hell. Islam has no reincarnation. Giving up your life for Allah is a sure way of getting your 72 virgins.

For many, Islam matches expectations about religion and deity. Islam holds to one supreme deity, worshipped through good deeds and disciplined religious rituals. After death, you receive reward or punishment according to your religious devotion. This is the Muslim's belief.

SUMMARY

In these major belief systems and their views of God, we find tremendous diversity:

- Hindus acknowledge multitudes of gods and goddesses.
- Buddhists recognize no deity.

- New Agers believe they are God.

- Muslims believe in a powerful but unknowable God.

- Christians believe in a loving and approachable God.

Are all religions worshiping the same God? New Age teaches that everyone should come to center on a cosmic consciousness, but that would require Muslims to give up their one God, Hindus to give up their numerous gods, and Buddhists to establish that God exists.

The world's major religions are each quite unique. Only one affirms a personal, loving God whom you know now, in this life. Jesus spoke of a God who welcomes us into a relationship with Him and comes alongside us as a comforter, counselor, and powerful God who loves us.

In Hinduism, you are on your own trying to gain release from karma. In New Age, you are working at your own divinity. In Buddhism, you have an individual quest for freedom from desire. And in Islam, you follow religious laws for the sake of paradise after death. With Jesus, you see a personal relationship with a personal God — a relationship that carries over into the next life.

Many world religions place you on your own, striving for spiritual perfection. Buddha, for example, never claimed to be sinless. Mohammed also admitted his need of forgiveness. No matter how wise, gifted, or influential other prophets, gurus, and teachers might be, they knew they were imperfect, just like the rest of us.

Many religions focus on your spiritual efforts. With Jesus, you have a two-way interaction with God. He welcomes us to go to him. *"The Lord is near to all who call upon him, to all who call upon him in truth"* (Psalm 145:18).

You can communicate with God, who will answer your prayer, give you greater peace and joy, provide direction, show you His love, and transform your life. Jesus said, *"I came that they might have life, and have it more abundantly"* (John 10:10). It will not make life perfect and free of problems. But in the midst of life, you can relate to God, who wants to be involved in your life and faithful in His love.

This is not a commitment to a method of self-improvement like the Eight-fold Path, the Five Pillars, meditation, good works, or even the Ten Commandments. These seem clear, easy-to-follow paths for spirituality. But they become a burden while striving for perfection, and God remains distant.

Our hope is not in following laws or standards, but in knowing a Savior who fully accepts us because of our faith in Him and His sacrifice for us. We don't earn our place in heaven by religious efforts or good deeds. Heaven is a free gift when we begin a relationship with Jesus.

This battlefront should be easy to fight. Remember, you are not attacking their faith, they are challenging yours. This act puts you in control. By a combination of your *"Killer Questions"* and the use of your absolute authority, the Bible, you can win this front. (If you're confronting an atheist, he'll be eager to dismiss other religions as false anyway.)

The next battlefront will be harder. *Why?* Now your adversary will use part of the Bible as his faith. Arm yourself for *"Is Jesus the only way to God? (Part 2)."*

IS JESUS THE ONLY WAY TO GOD? PART 2

(AQ) Questions you ask the Atheist to make him think)

RELIGIONS AND THE BIBLE

Two religions use the Bible as their source: Christianity and Judaism. Both use the same Old Testament to create some of their traditions. These traditions will later become doctrines.

TRADITIONS AND DOCTRINE

What are Tradition and Doctrine?

Tradition is *"the handing down of statements, beliefs, legends, customs, and information from generation to generation, especially by word of mouth or by practice."* This is a general description, but how do you apply this to theology?

Christians would call it *"a body of teachings, or any one of them, held to have originated from the Messiah and His apostles but not originally committed to writing."*

Jews would call it *"a body of laws and doctrines, or any one of them, held to have originated from Moses and originally handed down orally from generation to generation."*

The word doctrine, in religion, means, *"a body or system of teachings relating to a particular subject,"* or, *"a particular principle, position, or policy taught or advocated."*

Here lies the problem. If you misuse a tradition or Scripture, you will produce a doctrine in error. Believing the doctrine does not make it right. Goliath was a very sincere believer. In 1 Samuel 17:43, Goliath *"cursed David by his gods."* He has his doctrines, but they were in error.

SINCERITY IS NOT ENOUGH

Some argued that even if your religion is false, what really matters is your sincerity. My reply: *"That dog don't hunt."* This notion stems from a false belief that religion pleases God. The problem is that the Bible teaches that any religion that does not recognize YHVH is a direct rebellion against God.

Sincerity does not determine truth. You can be very sincere and yet sincerely wrong. For example, accidental deaths sometimes occur when patients receive the wrong prescription. Most of these cases involve no malice, but rather medical workers who mistakenly—but sincerely—administer the wrong treatment.

Sincerity never substitutes for the truth. Consider Mohammed, Adolf Hitler, ISIS, and the 9-11 hijackers. All were sincere in their beliefs to the extreme — even to death. God never accepts sincerity. He judges mankind on truth. That truth is Jesus, the Messiah.

Jesus did not claim that He was the *best* way to God but the *only* way. That's either totally true or totally false — salvation has no room for Jesus *and* some other Savior.

Critics call this a narrow-minded view. Here is the problem: just because the Messianic faith seems narrow, it does not become untrue. Truth itself is exclusive. If the Messianic faith is true, then we must accept the teachings of Jesus, who demands our total allegiance. Some would reject this as cruel and unloving; but the Bible teaches that you have any other ways to God, the Messiah died in vain (Galatians 2:21).

Some ask, "If the Messiah is the only way to God, what happens to those who have not heard?" I, as an atheist, used this question to try to destroy other people's faith in God.

This question is but a smokescreen you raise when you're trying to rationalize your own rejection of the Messiah. You imply that God lacks compassion for imposing His plan of salvation upon us all.

This would make you more compassionate then God. You assume that people are lost because they had not heard the gospel, but they are actually lost because of their sin of the rejection of God. Jesus is not the curse; Jesus is the cure.

You should not speculate beyond what the Bible says on this matter. God Himself determines what will happen to those who have not heard. God judges with perfect justice and will always do what is right.

Here is your problem: you have heard the good news, and now it is your choice. You must respond. He died for the world, but He cannot become your Lord and Savior until you accept Him.

After defusing the emotional bomb, you must move on to an important question of truth as we have discussed. Faith, no matter how sincere or intense, is no more valid than its object.

Facts are facts, regardless of your attitude toward them. The basic question is always, "Is it true?" We will deal with facts. Other religions may share some similarities, but the differences overpower them by far.

CHRISTIANITY

The five basic beliefs of the Christian faith are:

1. *The Virgin Birth*
2. *The Theory of Atonement*
3. *The Bodily Resurrection of the Messiah*

4. *The Miracles of Jesus*

5. *The Unerring Word of God*

Contemporary Christian spirituality tends to be individualistic. At churches or Christian events, many of the worship songs are in first-person singular, speaking about God and His goodness as a personal experience.

Pop Christian spirituality sometimes seems to be all about "me and Jesus," and this is often true in some parts of Messianic Judaism as well. Instead of confronting the alienation and isolation of twenty-first century life, the faith seems softened into a more livable version.

Once you, individually, have had a personal, undeniable, transformative encounter with God, community connection is optional. Thank God for that personal experience, but if you stop there, you miss a major component of spiritual life.

Jewish culture, on the other hand, religious or not, tends more to community, with an emphasis on belonging before believing. This sometimes deteriorates to belonging instead of believing. You can neglect the reality of your transformative encounter with God amid the riches of communal life and commitment.

In truth, the two are inseparable. For Messianic Jews, that community includes both the universal *ekklesia* (body of Messiah) and *klal Yisrael* (the Jewish people).

FALSE FORMS OF CHRISTIANITY

When we apply the fifth belief, "the unerring word of God," out of context and in error, we get false doctrine. Time creates a new tradition, which strengthens the false doctrine. Let's look at two doctrines. One will not affect your salvation, the other one can.

The "Seed Faith" Doctrine

This doctrine originated from Oral Roberts after World War II. He took Scripture verses from the Bible and creatively transformed (twisted) them into another gospel.

This doctrine teaches that you can use the Scriptures to win God's favor. Sometimes you will hear it called the "Prosperity Gospel" or "give to get." You should give generously in the *expectation* of receiving much more.

The main Scriptures used in this teaching are the following: *"Will a man rob God? Yet you are robbing Me! But you say, 'How have we robbed You?' In tithes and offerings"* (Malachi 3:8).

"Give, and it will be given to you. They will pour into your lap a good measure -pressed down, shaken together, and running

over. For by your standard of measure it will be measured to you in return" (Luke 6:38).

"Now this I say, he who sows sparingly will also reap sparingly, and he who sows bountifully will also reap bountifully" (2 Corinthians 9:6).

ALL of these motivations are wrong. God has ALWAYS wanted, and will judge, by a "willing heart." This doctrine takes these verses out of context.

Here is the answer for the willing heart: *"Each one must do just as he has purposed in his heart, not grudgingly or under compulsion, for God loves a cheerful giver. And God is able to make all grace abound to you, so that always having all sufficiency in everything, you may have an abundance for every good deed"* (2 Corinthians 9:7-8).

God will not allow you to use Him for "Give to Get." Look at Job 41:11 — *"Who has given me anything, and made me PAY him back? Everything belongs to me under all of Heaven."*

In Romans 11:35, Paul quotes Job: *"Or who hath given Him anything, and made Him pay it back?"* God's character will not allow Himself to become a "Hip Pocket Genie."

"Sow a seed of faith, reap a harvest of blessing." This and many other similar phrases fill the sermons of some pastors and televangelists today to manipulate their weaker brothers and sisters into giving.

The pastors' pocketbooks grow, but at great cost—the giver will lose faith when the expected blessing never comes. These audacious "spiritual leaders" don't seem to know Whom they're messing with. *"What do you mean by crushing my people, by grinding the face of the poor?' declares the Lord GOD of hosts"* (Isaiah 3:15).

The "Law" Distorted

Write down your answer to this question: When Paul is talking about the "Law" what "Law" does he mean? When you are finished, continue reading.

Without the context to that question, you cannot answer it correctly. Your mind went to your understanding of Paul's Law, and you placed it into a missing context. Here is why.

When Paul refers to "the Law," he gives seven of them. They are:

1. The Law of God (Romans 3:31; 7:22-25; 8:7)
2. The Law of Sin (Romans 7:23-25)
3. The Law of Sin and Death (Romans 8:2)
4. The Law of the Spirit of Life (Romans 8:2)
5. The Law of Faith (Romans 3:27)
6. The Law of Righteousness (Romans 9:11-12)
7. The Law of the Messiah (1 Corinthians 9:21)

God did not give the Law to answer the question: "What must I do to be saved?" OR "How can I have a relationship with God?" He gave it so you may know how to live out your life *after* you are saved — out of love.

Because of two thousand years of misguided teachings, we must correct a teaching. The word *Torah* does not mean "Law." It means, in Hebrew thought, "God's Instructions."

Paul did not abolish the Torah. But in order for God to regard it as good, the Law needed a grounding in trust, NEVER in legalism. When you realize Paul flatly rejected perverting the Torah into legalism and fully accepted the Torah itself, then the contradictions in his view of the Torah vanish.

Most Bible Scholars believe that the books of Romans and Galatians appeared AFTER the Council of Jerusalem (Acts 15), and BEFORE Paul followed the Torah at the request of James in Jerusalem (Acts 21).

We can prove Paul's theology through Galatians 2:16 — *"Knowing that a man is not justified by the works of the law, but by the faith of Jesus the Messiah, even we have believed in Jesus the Messiah, and not by the works of the law: for by the works of the law shall no flesh be justified."*

Most believers assume that *erga nomou* — literally, "works of law," a term that appears three times in this verse, must mean "actions done in obedience to the Torah." But this is wrong. A Gentile, the Reverend C.E.B. Cranfield, in his Commentary on the book of Romans, writes:

> *"...It will be well to bear in mind the fact that the Greek language of Paul's day possessed NO word-group corresponding to our 'Legalism', 'Legalist,' and 'Legalistic.'* (This had not received attention before it was noted in the Scottish Journal of Theology, Volume 17, 1964, page 55.) *This means that he lacked a convenient terminology for expressing a vital distinction, and so was surely seriously hampered in the work of clarifying the Messianic position with regard to the Law.*
>
> *In view of this, we should always be ready to reckon with the possibility that Pauline statements, which at first sight seem to dispurge the law, were really directed NOT against the law itself BUT against that misunderstanding and misuse of it for which we NOW have a convenient terminology. In this very difficult terrain, Paul was pioneering. If we make due allowance for these circumstances, we shall not be so easily baffled or misled by a certain impreciseness of statement which we shall sometimes encounter."* (C.E.B. Cranfield, *The International Critical Commentary, Romans,* 1979, page 853)

Was Paul a good teacher of the Word of God?

- If YES, we should follow what he says.

- If NO, it makes him a false teacher and a hypocrite, and we should reject what he says.

The answer to this question will determine your doctrine, just as it did Marcion, declared a heretic and excommunicated in 144 CE. His interpretation of Isaiah 45:7 was fundamental to his doctrine: *"I form the light, and create darkness: I make peace, and create evil: I the LORD do all these things."*

By this one verse, he reasoned that an evil tree cannot produce good fruit. So he concluded we must have two gods: the Creator God of the Old Testament, who was fickle and cruel, and the Supreme God of the New Testament, a God of love as revealed in Jesus. He rejected the entire Old Testament and only accepted the Gospel of Luke. Even then, he edited out all of Luke's references to the Old Testament. His gospel, had no prophecies or Jewish historical events.

For Marcion, the only true apostle was Paul. He believed the other apostles had corrupted Jesus' teachings by adding legalism. He took ten of Paul's epistles, excluding 1 and 2 Timothy and Titus, and removed any verse showing "Jewish corruptions." This is how he handled Paul's concept of the "Law."

Some people, like Marcion, ignore or forget some Scriptures while creating doctrines from others. This creates an unbalanced view of the Word of God. How can the Old Testament be "old" when 78% of it is unfulfilled? How can the New Testament be "new" when 96% of its quotations come from the Old Testament?

Consider these verses:

Con	Pro
Ephesians 2:15: The "Law" (Torah) is Abolished	Romans 3:31: The "Law" (Torah) has been Established
Romans 7:6: We have been "Discharged from the Law" (Torah)	Romans 7:12: The "Law (Torah) is Holy, just and good" (Note: This statement is in the same chapter)
Romans 10:4: The Messiah is "the END of the Law (Torah)"	Romans 8:3-4: The Just Requirements of the Law (Torah) is "fulfilled in us"
Romans 3:28: The "Law (Torah) is unnecessary"	1 Corinthians 7:19: The "Law (Torah) is necessary" Note: This can also be found in Ephesians 6:2-3 and 1 Timothy 1:8-10)
2 Corinthians 3:7: The Law (Torah) is the "Dispensation of Death"	Romans 3:2: The Law (Torah) is part of "The Oracles of G-d" entrusted to the Jews

All of these Scriptures flow from the writings of one man, Paul, to one group of people — Gentiles. You cannot use these verses against the Jewish people. You will be "reading someone else's mail."

If you feel that Paul was all things to all people so that he might win some, you have made Paul a hypocrite and a false teacher.

Paul was a good teacher. When you read the Scriptures in context, you will find Paul dealing with two types of believers:

1)   Gentile believers and their salvation (CON). These are verses connected to Salvation (Justification or "Right standing before God."). Paul was teaching against the idea that salvation requires "Jesus PLUS_____(fill in the blank)."

In all of Paul's writings to the Gentiles, the word *justification* appears over eighty times, but he never uses the word *repentance*. He applies this word only to Jews. — *WHY?*

Repentance implies "returning to where you came from." For Gentiles that would require going back to idol worship.

2)   Gentile believers and their Conduct.-PRO. This deals with the believer's conduct after salvation. (Sanctification or "Right Living before God.")

Jesus said to "make disciples of all nations." A disciple follows the teachings and the life of his master — In our case, Jesus. He followed the "LAW." (Torah-God's Instructions and teachings). Paul applied this process to the Gentiles.

Gentiles, somehow, through some mystery have their identities changed: *"but now in the Messiah Jesus you who have once were far of way have been brought near through the blood of the Messiah"* (Ephesians 2:13). A radical transformation has occurred.

This is equivalent to the legal transformation that occurs when a Gentile converts to Judaism. Paul emphasized that the Gentile believers have received this new identity without a formal ritual conversion. *"Not by works lest any man boast,"* he said in Ephesians 2:9.

By *works* he meant the conventional conversion ritual, complete with the works of circumcision, immersion, and sacrifice. Instead we receive salvation "by grace…through faith."

According to Paul, Jesus destroyed the wall of separation — the barrier between the people of the nations and the people of God.

Because Jesus abolished the enmity, He has removed the dividing wall. Gentiles are free to move into the court of Israel. There they get free access to the Torah life that identifies Israel and to the House of God.

JUDAISM

What is Judaism? What does it mean to be a Jew? Most people, both Jewish and Gentile, would say that Judaism is a religion. Yet, some militant atheists insist that they are Jews! Is Judaism a race? If you think so, most Jews would call you an anti-Semite!

A Religion?

The religion called Judaism has a set of ideas about the world and how we should live our lives. You will learn about it in religious studies courses, and Jewish children study it in Hebrew schools. Certain aspects of those beliefs have great flexibility and disagreement about specifics, but that's part of the organized system of belief that is Judaism.

However, many people who call themselves Jews do not believe in that religion at all! More than half of all Jews in Israel today call themselves *secular* and don't believe in God or any Jewish religious beliefs. Half of all Jews in the United States don't belong to any synagogue. As a secular Jew, you may practice some of the rituals of Judaism and celebrate some of the holidays, but you don't think of these actions as religious activities.

Yet most Jews would agree that you're still a Jew, regardless of your disbelief. Clearly, then, being Jewish comprises more than just a religion.

A Race?

In the 1980s, the United States Supreme Court ruled that Jews are a race, at least for purposes of certain anti-discrimination laws. Their reasoning: at the time, people routinely spoke of the "Jewish race" as effortlessly as the "Italian race" or the "Negro race." That is what the legislators intended to protect.

That decision offended many Jews. *Why?* The idea of Jews as a race recalls nightmarish visions of Nazi Germany, which declared Jews not just a race, but an inferior one. The Nazi authorities rounded Jews up into ghettos and exterminated them like vermin.

This may offend some, but Jews are clearly not a race. Race is a genetic distinction, requiring shared ancestry. You can't change your race; it's in your DNA. I could never become black or Asian no matter how much I might want to.

Common ancestry is not required to be a Jew, though many Jews worldwide do share it. You can become a Jew by converting—just because you want to. I could never become black or Asian, but blacks and Asians have become Jews, like Sammy Davis, Jr., and Connie Chung.

A Culture / Ethnic Group?

Most secular American Jews think of their Jewishness as a matter of culture or ethnicity. Jewish culture would represent the food, the Yiddish language, some limited holiday observances, and cultural values like the emphasis on education.

Yet much of this is just the culture of Ashkenazic Jews, whose ancestors come from one particular region. Jews have lived in many parts of the world and have developed many different traditions.

Another Jewish culture is Sephardic. They have neither Yiddish nor are bagels and lox, chopped liver, latkes, gefilte fish, nor matzah ball soup part of this culture. As a Sephardic, your idea of Jewish cooking includes bourekas, phyllo dough pastries filled with cheese or spinach. Your ancestors probably wouldn't know what to do with a dreidel.

Despite cultural traits and behaviors shared by many Jews, Judaism must be something more than a culture or an ethnic group.

A Nation?

The traditional explanation, and the one given in the Torah, is that the Jews are a nation. The Hebrew word is *goy*. Today it implies a territorial and political entity, but the Torah and the rabbis used this term to mean a group of people with a common history, a common destiny, and a sense of interconnection.

Unfortunately, in modern times, we have contaminated the term *nation* with ugly notions of a country obsessed with its own superiority and bent on world domination. Some accuse non-Israeli Jews of disloyalty to their own country in favor of their loyalty to the "Jewish nation," which may mean Israel or the worldwide body of Jews.

Some used this distorted interpretation of *nationhood* to prove that Jews control the world (or seek to). Because of this, *nation*, is no longer appropriate to describe the Jewish people.

A Family?

Almost all Jews feel an inexplicable sense of interconnectedness. Traditionally, we understood this as "nationhood" or "peoplehood."

The Bible and Jewish literature refer to the Jewish people as "the Children of Israel," a reference to the fact that we are all the physical or spiritual descendants of the patriarch Jacob, who was later called Israel. We are part of his extended family.

As a member of the Jewish "family," you don't always agree with all of your "siblings." You often argue and criticize each other. You hold each other to the very highest standards, knowing that the shortcomings of your brother will reflect badly on all of you. But when an outsider unfairly criticizes your family or any part thereof, you quickly join together in opposition.

When your "cousins" suffer hardship or persecution, you all feel the pain. For example, in the 1980s, when droughts and famines plagued Africa, you may have learned for the first time about the Beta Israel, the Jews of Ethiopia. Their religion, race and culture are quite different from yours—not to mention thitherto unknown. And yet, your heart ached for them as your fellow Jews during this period of famine. Jews from around the world helped them to immigrate to Israel.

When your "kin" does something illegal, immoral or shameful, you all feel the shame. You were all shocked at the assassination of Israeli Prime Minister Yitzchak Rabin by a

Jew. You couldn't believe that one Jew would ever kill another.

You also take pride in those who reflect the best of your family — scientists like Albert Einstein or political leaders like Joe Lieberman. (You may not agree with his politics or his religious views, but you were all proud to see him on a national ticket).

JEWISH TRADITIONS

As an Orthodox Jew, you follow a number of traditions. For example: Nowhere does the Talmud teach that you should not follow the Sabbath, but rabbis can have disagreements on how you follow this Scripture:

*"For six days work (**avodah**) may be done, but on the seventh day you shall have a holy day, a sabbath of complete rest to the LORD; whoever does any work (**malachah**) on it shall be put to death"* (Exodus 35:2).

Note two different Hebrew words to represent work. MALACHAH stresses creative work. Usual work is AVODAH. In the context of Exodus 35, MALACHAH specifically concerns work performed in the construction of the Tabernacle.

The rabbis took this verse and constructed 39 categories of *malachah* work used in the construction of the Tabernacle

(Mishkan) and prohibited them on the Sabbath. This listing has become the basis of most of the common Sabbath laws practiced among the Orthodox Jews today.

Listed below are these 39 categories and their purposes:

1) Plowing
2) Planting
3) Harvesting
4) Gathering
5) Threshing
6) Sifting, Purpose: To grow and process plants needed to make dyes to color the wool and skins used in the Mishkan.
7) Selecting
8) Winnowing
9) Grinding
10) Kneading *
11) Baking *
12) Shearing
13) Bleaching
14) Dyeing
15) Spinning
16) Weaving
17) Combing
19) Threading a Loom
20) Threading a Harness
21) Tying a Knot
22) Untying a Knot
23 Sewing
24 Tearing

(*-The Jerusalem Talmud holds that the purpose of kneading and baking were to prepare the 12 "Show-Breads."), Purpose: To prepare the wool and weave it into curtains.

25) Trapping   26) Slaughtering

27) Skinning   28) Tanning, Purpose: To prepare the skins for the Mishkan covering.

29) Smoothing   30) Marking

31) Cutting to a Shape

32) Writing 2 Letters

33) Erasing 2 Letters, Purpose: To rebuild the Mishkan properly, they wrote letters were written on the courtyard pillars to identify their position. Letters were often erased and rewritten.

34) Building

35) Demolishing, Purpose: To assemble and disassemble the Mishkan when traveling.

36) Kindling a Fire

37) Extinguishing a Fire, Purpose: To light the fires needed for dyeing the wool and smelting the metals and to produce charcoal.

38) Final Hammer Blow (Completing), Purpose: To complete the metal construction.

39) Carrying, Purpose: To move the pillars from the wagons to a public area and vice versa; To bring the tithes from the tents to a public area.

From these 39 categories came thousands of rules. Here is an example, using category 39 (carrying):

If a woman has a bobby pin in her hair, is she wearing it or carrying it? The rabbis say she is wearing it, which means she is not breaking the Sabbath.

If a man has his car keys in his pocket, is he wearing them or carrying them? The rabbis say he is carrying, breaking the Sabbath.

If the keys were attached to a belt loop on his pants, is he wearing them or carrying them? The rabbis say wearing and not breaking the Sabbath.

Jesus' disagreement with the Jewish leaders came from these 39 categories. An example is John 5:1-16. He healed the man unable to walk with these words: *"...Rise, take up thy bed and walk."* (verse 8) Thus, He told a man to break this category on the Sabbath.

MESSIANIC JUDAISM

Here I must remind the reader that I, an ex-atheist, am now an ordained Messianic Jewish minister.

These are the seven levels of modern Judaism:

Secular: You celebrate traditional Jewish holidays as historical and nature festivals and mark life events such as births, marriages, and deaths in a secular manner. Your Jewishness operates as a race, not a religion.

Reconstructionist: Created from the Zionist movement, this attaches to the land of Israel. You commit to social justice and personal ethics. You will follow traditional Halakha, but religion has no binding authority on you.

Reformed (aka Liberal or Progressive, founded in 1825): You emphasize the evolving nature of the religion and the superiority of its ethical aspects over the ceremonial ones. You believe in a continuous revelation not centered on the presence of God at Mount Sinai. You hold closer to traditions.

Conservative: You adhere to the Torah and Talmud but allow for some departures to keep up with differing times and circumstances.

Orthodox: You adhere faithfully to the principles and practices of traditional Judaism. You show this chiefly by a devotion to and study of the Torah, daily synagogue attendance if possible, and strict observance of the Sabbath, religious festivals, holy days, and the dietary laws.

Haredim (aka strictly Orthodox or Ultra-Orthodox): You are in a broad spectrum of groups within Orthodox Judaism. You reject modern secular culture.

Messianic: You combine the Halakha (walk) elements of Reformed and Orthodox Judaism, Jewish traditions, and the Christian belief that Jesus is the Messiah.

Paul never makes an argument for Israel's presence in the Church. Israel joining to the Church. The gospel does not make Jews into Gentiles. Paul's theology has Gentiles entering the Kingdom of Israel, joining Israel as fellow citizens. We are strangers brought near; we are Israel by faith. Jew and Gentile join together, like the two halves of Ezekiel's stick, to make one new man.

Isaiah 56:6-7 says, *"Also the sons of the stranger, that join themselves to the LORD, to serve him, and that love the name of the LORD, to be his slaves, every one that keeps from polluting the Sabbath, and takes hold of my covenant; even them will I bring to the mountain of my holiness, and refresh them in the house of my prayer: their burnt offerings and their sacrifices shall be accepted upon my altar; for my house shall be called, House of prayer for all peoples."*

Gentile believers have a legitimate place in the Israel of God.

Isaiah also tells us that the nations will keep the Sabbath. The nations will keep the covenant of Torah. The Lord will accept their burnt offerings and sacrifices on the His altar. Together, Jew and Gentile will worship before the Lord on the monthly new moons (the Feasts) and the weekly Sabbaths:

""*From one new moon to another and from one Shabbat to another, all mankind will come and bow before me,' says the Lord"* (Isaiah 66:23).

The Orthodox and Messianic Separation (90-95 CE)

The Pharisees began a policy of exclusion: "Either play by our rules or we don't let you play at all." They added a 19th blessing to the Amidah prayer, the 18 benedictions spoken daily by observant Jews.

The 19th Benediction (the "Birkhat haMinim") is the blessing on heretics. Messianic Jews would not say this blessing to avoid cursing themselves. Thus, the Pharisees immediately expelled them from the synagogue. Freshly expelled, the Messianic Believers opened new Synagogues and the Gentiles.

Five changes became set in Law at this time. They remain within the Jewish faith today.

1) Two Torahs (Written and Oral).
2) Authority of the Rabbis (What they say in religious matters is binding).
3) Irrational interpretation (Midrashic; creative).
4) Man-made Laws (enactment of new Laws).

5) Traditions of Men (Customs become binding as Law).

The Bar Kochba War (132-135 CE)

Hadrian became emperor in 117 CE. In 132 CE, he wanted to rebuild the Temple to contain Zeus, king of the Greek gods. This threatened the very existence of the Jewish people. This was the start of the Bar Kochba War. Rabbi Akiva, rabbi of his day and the head of the Sanhedrin, declared Bar Kochba the Messiah. This created a firestorm of debate between the rabbis and forced the Messianic Believers to leave.

In 135 CE, Bar Kochba was killed at Betar, and Rabbi Akiva was skinned alive. Rome rebuilt Jerusalem and renamed it "Aelia Capitolina." *Aelia* reflected the second name of Hadrian (Publius Aelius Hadrianus). It indicated the city's dedication to imperial worship. *Capitolina* reminded the Jews that the city would also dedicate itself to the worship of the Roman gods of the Capitoline Hill— Jupiter, Minerva, and Juno). A temple to Jupiter (Satan) rose on Mount Zion, desecrating the site of the Holy Temple.

The Jews could not enter the city under penalty of death. Hope faded for Jewish independence and rebuilding the Temple. Defeated, the Jewish nation dispersed. Without the

Temple, they could not continue to observe of Israel's feasts outlined in the Torah.

This produced the first Gentile leader of the Messianic movement which would become known as the Church. Without Jewish influence, wrong doctrines began to take its place.

Jesus' Gentile Lineage Connection

Any good Bible student knows that Jesus' lineage is from the line of David, the King of Israel. You may not know is that His line includes three Gentiles.

Tamar (Genesis 38)

According to *All the Women in the Bible* (Chapter 2, Zondervan), Tamar was a Canaanite. In the story of Tamar and Judah in Genesis 38, Judah acted out of sensual lust alone. Tamar had nobler motives, though—namely, to become the mother of Judah's tribal representative. Twin sons came from that scandalous union—Perez, and Zerah. Through Perez, Judah and Tamar became ancestors of Jesus.

God's election is only by grace, otherwise He would never have chosen Judah. He was a Jew; Tamar, a Gentile. Thus their parentage of Perez (Matthew 1:3) foreshadows how both Jews and Gentiles would share in the blessings of God's Word.

Ruth 4:18-22 says, *"This, then, is the family line of Perez: Perez was the father of Hezron, Hezron the father of Ram, Ram the father of Amminadab, Amminadab the father of Nahshon, Nahshon the father of Salmon, Salmon the father of Boaz, Boaz the father of Obed, Obed the father of Jesse, and Jesse the father of David."*

Prostitution did not give birth to Perez, but rather the asserted claim of levirate marriage being.

When Judah says of Tamar, *"She is more righteous than I,"* he becomes a redeemer, not only in the legal sense of the levirate, but also in the ethical-Messianic sense: Judah has redeemed Tamar's action for the good.

Tamar's redeeming act provides the opportunity, the impulse, and the need for Judah to become a redeemer. Perez is great, great, great, great, grandfather of Boaz, who is the great grandfather of David.

Rahab, the Harlot

The first part of *Rahab*, "Ra," was the name of an Egyptian god. As an Amorite, Rahab belonged to an idolatrous people. Her name meant "insolence, fierceness, or broad spaciousness."

Some of the ancient sages said that she became the wife of Joshua, but in the royal genealogy of Jesus, Rahab appears as the wife of Salmon, one of the two spies she sheltered. In turn, she became the mother of Boaz, who married Ruth.

Rahab, the one-time heathen harlot, married into one of the leading families of Israel and became an ancestress of our Lord. She is the only woman listed by name among the heroes of faith in Hebrews 11 (verse 31).

Despite her sanctified name, Hebrews James (James 2:25) still labeled her as Rahab the harlot. She still carried the evil name and title, thus declaring the unique grace of the transforming power of God.

She believed with the heart (Romans 10:9-10), confessed with the mouth, and acted on her profession at the risk of her life. Rahab is a fitting illustration of another miracle of God's divine grace—calling forth His congregation out of a godless, gentile world.

Scripture has two genealogies of Jesus. The first genealogy in Luke 3:32 reads *"who was the son of Jesse, who was the son of Obed, who was the son of Boaz, who was the son of Salmon, who was the son of Naasson,..."*

The second is written in Matthew 1:5 –6, *"Salmon begat Boaz of* **Rachab** *((KJ)* **Rahab** *(ASV)); Boaz begat Obed of Ruth; Obed begat Jesse; Jesse begat David the king;..."*

What was the name of Boaz's mother? It was Rahab, the harlot of Jericho.

Ruth, the Moabitess

According to Jewish teachings, Ruth was a granddaughter of Eglon, king of Moab, who himself was a grandson of Balak, king of Moab during Moses' time. Both had hostile relations with the Israelites: Balak retained Balaam to curse the Israelites (Numbers 22-24); Eglon allied with the Ammonites and Amalekites and occupied Israel for eighteen years until slain by the Israeli leader, Ehud. (Judges 3).

Where did the Moabites come from? Moab is the son of Lot by one of his own daughters. Ruth's ancestry had its origin in incest. Though related to the Israelites, the Moabites were enemies because Moab had opposed Israel's advance toward Canaan. Moabites did not worship YHVH. They were pagans, occasionally offering human sacrifices to idol-gods like Chemosh.

As a result, God prohibited the Jews from intermingling and intermarrying with Moabites (Ezra 9:10-12)—unless a Moabite renounced all Moabite-ness and became a Jew.

Ruth was a descendant of Moab. Boaz, who became Ruth's redeemer-husband, was the son of Rahab (Ruth 4:21, 1 Chronicles 2:11, Matthew 1:5).

Imagine the stories Boaz heard as he grew up. His mother had been a foreigner and a harlot, yet she grafted into the olive tree of Israel by the grace of God. This affected the way Boaz viewed Ruth that day he saw her gleaning in his field.

Other men might have simply seen a foreign woman scrounging for food, like a parasite. Boaz, however, saw something familiar and dear. This woman who had left her family, her nation, and her gods, to embrace the Hebrew Naomi, her nation, and her God. This was his childhood.

If the Messiah will redeem the whole world from evil and make it work for good, He ought to come from the house of David. Not only Jews but non-Jews must enter His line and contribute to a redemption that enters His birthright and inheritance.

Ruth is no longer a Moabite idolater when she says, *"Your God will be my God."* Then she can become the great-grandmother of David. A canonical book of the Old Testament is named after a Moabite woman. This is itself a testimony to a miracle of God's grace.

God had uniquely prepared Boaz for Ruth and Ruth for Boaz. It was a marriage made in heaven. (Jew and Gentile). Their union produced a son named Obed, who had a son named Jesse, who had a son named David, who became the greatest king Israel ever had. That is until David's progeny produced a King named Jesus.

God weaves His grace throughout the Bible—even through the genealogies!

Like Vietnam veterans, Messianic Jews have often felt scorned by both Jews and Christians alike, as if being loyal to both our God and our Messiah is a sin.

To go on this walk, both Jew and Gentile had to go against tradition for the sake of Truth.

- For the Gentile, rebuilding the wall of the Law that crumbled when Jesus rose from the dead.

- For the Jew, Worshipping a false God and a traitor to His people.

Our believing brethren should understand that our faith in Jesus has caused us:

- As a Jew, to rediscover just how Jewish we are.

- As a Gentile, to rediscover our Jewish roots, our love of YHVH, and our love and respect for His Jewish people.

We will all be keeping the biblical calendar in the Messiah's Kingdom. In that day, all mankind will keep the seventh-day, biblical Sabbath and God's feasts. When we sit down to eat with the Master, the only menu options will be kosher.

If Messianic Jerusalem is our final destination, we don't have to wait until we arrive there to live that way. We can become Jew and Gentile today — one New Man in Messiah!

The final great move of God with His people is in Revelation 14:12 — *"Here is the patience of the saints, who keep the commandments of God and the faith of Jesus (Yeshua)"*.

Is this not the Living Word (Jesus) building His Living Bridge (Jew and Gentile) in the hearts of His People (His Temple)?

SUMMARY: IS YOUR FAITH VALID?

The seven types of faith are:

1. Common Faith (Brings you into the Kingdom) Titus 1:4

2. Little Faith (teaches you to trust) Matthew 8:26

3. Temporary Faith (Most critical–can go up or down) Luke 8:13

4. Strong Faith (refuses defeat) Romans 4:18-22

5. Creative Faith, also known as Great Faith (recognizing the authority of God) Matthew 8:10

6. Active Faith (the power of confessing the Word) James 1:22-25

7. Divine Faith (full trust and faith in God) Galatians 3:22

Reject the idea that "it doesn't matter what you believe as long as you believe it." Hitler slaughtered of six million Jews in a sincere view of race supremacy, but he was desperately wrong. What we believe must be true in order to be real. Jesus said, *"I am the way, the truth, and the life. No man cometh unto the father but by Me"* (John 14:6).

We can come to the Messiah by many ways, but He is the only way to know the true and living God in personal experience — the *only* way to God.

An atheist might claim that the believer's experience is sometimes harmful. "Look at all the religious nuts in mental asylums. It's their religion that put them there."

If this is your belief, you have succumbed to the "common-factor fallacy." An old story tells of a man who got drunk each Monday on whiskey and soda water; on Tuesday, he got drunk on brandy and soda water; and on Wednesday and on gin and soda water. What caused the drunkenness? Obviously, it was the common factor, soda water!

Is Jesus the only way to God? I believe I have shown that He is. At the same time, I could not leave this subject without completely destroying the idea of an alternate Messiah.

This is a common defense that I used as an atheist. I could not devote just a paragraph or two to this subject. It required an entire chapter: *"Mithra and Jesus."*

MITHRA AND JESUS

INTRODUCTION

In my other life as an atheist, I used the knowledge in this chapter to destroy people's faith. God changed that process.

1 John 2:18 reads, *"My children, it is the latter time; and as ye have heard that a false Messiah was to arise, so there are now many false Messiahs; and from this we know that it is the latter time."*

One of these false Messiahs at that time called himself *"the divine sun"* — Mithra or Mithras. If you use the Roman god *Mithra* to claim Jesus did not exist, history will prove you wrong.

If an atheist uses this framework to destroy your faith, he will have one of two reasons:

1) Ignorance. You can use this chapter will remove it.
2) He knows it's a lie. You must avoid using another lie to back your faith. This will make your belief indefensible.

With this understanding, let's take a look at the framework.

THE FRAMEWORK

Mainstream scholarship lists at least three Mithras: Mitra, the Vedic god; Mithra, the Indo-Persian deity; and Mithras, the Greco-Roman god. The last two are particularly significant because of their relationship to early Christianity.

The worship of Mithra goes back over 3500 years. This god, a solar deity, originated as *Mitra* in the Indian Vedic religion. When the Iranians separated from their Indian brethren, Mitra changed to *Mithra*, the light and power behind the sun. By around 1500 BCE, Mithra worship had made it to the Near East, where Greece and later Rome would adopt it.

According to Clement of Rome's debate with Appion (*Homily* VI, ch. X), Mithra is also Apollo. The priests (*sacerdotes*), worshippers (*cultores*), and temples (*templum*) of the same deity show that Mithra was a Roman sun god. The Roman legionnaires called Mithra — or *Mithras* — "*the divine Sun, the Unconquered Sun.*"

An inscription found around 80 to 100 CE in Rome dedicates an altar to *"Sol Invictus Mithras"* — The Unconquered Sun Mithra.

MITHRA IN ROMAN HISTORY

Before the military campaign of Alexander the Great, Mithra became the favorite deity of Asia Minor. Rome absorbed this during Pompey's military campaign around 70 BCE. Through the soldiers, Mithras came into Rome.

Mithraism's theology gained much of its shape between 80 and 120 CE. This is also the timeframe of John's letters. It reached a peak during the second and third centuries. *How?*

On October 28, 312, a battle took place between the emperor of the Eastern Roman Empire, Maxentius, and Constantine, the emperor of the Western Roman Empire. Constantine won the battle and started on the path becoming the sole ruler of the Roman Empire. Constantine was a believer in Mithra, and he would mix part of this theology with Christianity at the Council of Nicaea in 325CE.

MITHRA AND JESUS

Before I continue, I must make two points.

1. The following comparison is solely the product of Gentile Christians, not the Jewish faiths. (Note: for the rest of this chapter, "Christian" or "Christianity" will refer strictly to *Gentiles* — Christian believers and converts who did not come from a Jewish background.)

2. I am not "Church bashing." If you are Christian, I could easily use the following information to attack your faith and make you doubt its very foundation. (I used to do that all the time as an atheist.) Make sure you read to the end if an atheist or agnostic tries to shake you. You will want all the facts.

Let's continue. Over the centuries — in fact, from the earliest Christian times — scholars have compared Mithraism to Christianity. *Why?* We find numerous similarities between their doctrines and traditions.

The following list represents a combination of them all for ease of reference. They suggest possible Mithraism influences upon Christianity.

As an atheist, I have compared Mithra with Jesus in the following ways:

- Mithra was born on December 25th of the virgin Anahita.
- She wrapped him in swaddling clothes and placed him in a manger, and shepherds attended.
- The Romans considered him a great traveling teacher and master.
- He had 12 companions or *disciples*.
- He performed miracles.

- As the "great bull of the Sun," Mithra sacrificed himself for world peace.

- Buried in a tomb, he rose again after three days. His followers celebrated this event each year at the time of Mithras' resurrection (and this date later became "Easter.")

- He ascended to heaven.

- His followers viewed Mithra as the Good Shepherd, the *"Way, the Truth and the Light,"* the Redeemer, Savior, and Messiah.

- Mithra is omniscient, as he "hears all, sees all, and knows all: none can deceive him."

- He identifies with both the Lion and the Lamb.

- His sacred day was Sunday, "the Lord's Day," hundreds of years before the appearance of the Messiah.

- His religion had a Eucharist or "Lord's Supper."

- Mithra "sets his marks on the foreheads of his soldiers."

- Mithraism emphasized baptism.

Does these comparisons stand in the light of history? **No.** Continue reading.

PERSIAN WINTER FESTIVALS

This festival of the winter solstice was also called the annual *rebirth, renewal,* or *resurrection* of the sun. Christmas (December 25) is not the birth of the son of God but of the *sun.* Pagans celebrated the winter solstice was centuries before Christ in numerous parts of the world. Christianity took it over, not as biblical doctrine but as a later tradition in order to compete with the Pagan cults.

MITHRA THE 'ROCK-BORN'

Mithra's birth came out of a rock followed by his adoration by shepherds. The early Christian father Jerome tells us that the cave shown at Bethlehem as the birthplace of Jesus was actually a rock shrine for the god Tammuz or Adonis. Christians adopted it as Jesus' birthplace as one of those frequent instances of "Christianizing" a pagan sacred site.

THE VIRGIN MOTHER, ANAHITA

The worship of Mithra and Anahita, his virgin mother, was common as early as 558 BCE. The book *Mithraism and Christianity*, portrays the Mithra myth in this way: *"According to Persian mythology, Mithras was born of a virgin given the title 'Mother of God.'"*

EARLY CHRUCH FATHERS ON MITHRAISM

Mithraism was so popular in the Roman Empire and so similar in important aspects to Christianity that several Church fathers had to address it, disparagingly of course.

These fathers included Justin Martyr, Tertullian, Julius Firmicus Maternus, and Augustine, all of whom attributed these striking coincidences to the devil. Supposedly Satan, anticipating the Messiah, set about to fool the Pagans by imitating the coming Messiah. In reality, the Church fathers confirm that these characteristics, traditions, and myths predated Christianity.

Christianity borrowed from the devil's book when it fixed the birth of the Savior on the December 25. Without doubt, that day was the traditional pagan birthday of the sun. The Church, as an afterthought, arbitrarily transferred the Nativity of its founder, Jesus, from January 6 to December 25.

CLAIMS VS TRUTH

A significant portion of the above claims about Mithras are simply *false*. Let's separate truth from fiction.

Claim: The Romans considered Mithras a great traveling teacher and master. *Is this true?*

Truth: Nothing in the Mithraic tradition indicates he was a teacher of *any* kind, but he could have been a master of sorts. This would be normal of *any* deity, however. Most mythologies describe their gods in this way.

Claim: Mithras had twelve companions or disciples. *Is this true?*

Truth: Nothing suggests this in the traditions of Iran or Rome. It is possible the idea developed from murals in which Mithras stands surrounded by twelve signs and personages of the Zodiac (two of whom are the moon and the sun). Because of the timeframe, it could have borrowed from Christianity.

Claim: Mithras promised his followers immortality. *Is this true?*

Truth: Little evidence exists for this, but Mithras might reasonably have offered immortality. This is common for any mythical deity.

Claim: Mithras performed miracles.

Truth: This is true but common for mythological characters.

Claim: Mithras sacrificed himself for world peace. *Is this true?*

Truth: We find little or no evidence for this, save for a story about Mithras slaying a threatening bull in a heroic deed. But that's as close as it gets.

Claim: Mithras lay dead in a tomb and after three days rose again, and his followers celebrated him each year at the time of his resurrection (later to become Easter in 165 CE by Pope Soter). *Is this true?*

Truth: Nothing in the Mithraic tradition indicates he ever even died, let alone resurrected. A Church father, Tertullian, did write about Mithraic believers re-enacting resurrection scenes, but well after New Testament times. Christianity could not, therefore, have borrowed from Mithraic traditions, but the opposite could certainly be true.

Claim: Followers called Mithras "the Good Shepherd" and identified him with both the Lamb and the Lion. *Is this true?*

Truth: We find *no* evidence that anyone called Mithras "the Good Shepherd" or identified him with a lamb. Since Mithras was a sun god, though, he has an association with Leo (the House of the Sun in Babylonian astrology). This could associate him with a lion. But all of this evidence comes after the New Testament; Mithraic believers again borrowed this attribute from Christianity.

Claim: Mithras was considered to be the "Way, the Truth and the Light," and the Logos, Redeemer, Savior, and Messiah. *Is this true?*

Truth: Based on the researched and known historic record of the Mithraic traditions, none of these terms has ever applied to Mithras, with the exception of *mediator*. But here is the problem: This term was used in a very different way from Christianity. Mithras was not the mediator between God and man but between the good and evil gods of Zoroaster.

Claim: Mithraic believers celebrated Sunday as Mithras' sacred day (also known as the "Lord's Day"). *Is this true?*

Truth: This tradition of celebrating Sunday is only true of Mithraic believers in Rome, and it dates from *post-*Messiah times. Once again, it likely came from Christianity rather than the other way around.

Claim: Mithraic believers celebrated a Eucharist or "Lord's Supper." *Is this true?*

Truth: Followers of Mithras did *not* celebrate a Eucharist, but they did celebrate a fellowship meal regularly, just as did many other groups in the Roman world.

As you can see, this quick examination shows Mithras isn't much like Jesus after all. It's not unusual for atheists to exaggerate the characteristics of Mithras in an effort to make them sound like Jesus.

If you are a believer, how would you fight these claims? The first step in refuting these claims is to investigate the attributes carefully.

Many alleged similarities between the pre-Roman mythologies and Jesus are extremely general and normal from anyone considering the existence of a divine creator. As Paul recognized on Mars Hill (Acts 17:22-31), men thought deeply about the nature of God prior to Jesus. Sometimes they imagined the details correctly; sometimes they didn't.

Similarities between Jesus and mythological gods fail to invalidate the history of Jesus. The historical truth of Jesus comes from the evidence and reliable eyewitness accounts. *Does that exist with Mithras?* **No.**

While Mithras no longer has worshipers, Christianity continues to thrive. *Why?* Their records are reliable. Also, the reliable Biblical record establishes the deity of Jesus in a way no other ancient mythological text could ever hope to achieve.

Does your atheist friend claim that Christianity just borrowed Jesus from the pagan god/man myths of the Near

East in the time of the Roman Empire? He is using "junk scholarship." *Why?* Three reasons:

First: The actual writings of the actual religions will show that these supposed parallels are either completely nonexistent or so trivial as to become virtually meaningless.

Second: All these other religions involve purely mythological demigods, not real people. By the Bible and secular ancient writings, we know where Jesus was born, where he lived, and where, when, and how he died. We know the name of his mother, father, cousin, aunt, uncle, and more that 25 of his best friends. The Gospels recorded His life within 50 years after His resurrection.

Who is Mithra? Nearly everything we know of this religion comes from writings hundreds of years AFTER Jesus lived. *What does that mean?* Logically, if anyone borrowed from anyone, Mithraism borrowed from Christianity — which, by the fourth century, had become the largest religion in the Roman Empire.

Third: The New Testament authors have every conceivable mark of reliability. Nearly all of them became martyrs for their faith. The very idea that Jews would create a religion out of other Near Eastern religions is absurd. *Again, how is that for "junk scholarship?"*

What about the similarities of moral teachings in different religions? You will find at least some moral "truth" in all human-generated religions. God gave us all a conscience and an awareness of right and wrong. However, the dualistic theology of Mithraism is diametrically opposed to Christian/Messianic theology.

When an atheist gives you words in scripture that Mithra said, ask for sources. Historians will want to know about these sources. *Why?* The Mithraic cult never wrote down their teachings, so we have very little evidence to help reconstruct its doctrine.

Also, as a believer, you have five points to consider when someone uses this process to destroy your trust in God.

1) Look for Loaded Language

Notice if any mini-god is called a *messiah* and was *baptized*, had *disciples* and a *ministry*. All of these terms favor the listener because they are Jewish or Christian concepts.

The Egyptians would never use these words to refer to their religious rites. The word *messiah* had a very specific meaning to the Jews, including being a descendant of David. It wasn't any political figure. Christianity teaches that believers are baptized only once; it is not simply a pre-religious washing ceremony. By mislabeling other deities with Christian terms, atheists can deluded you into believing the similarities are closer than they really are.

2) Ask, *"Can I read the source of these myths?"*

This is the single easiest way to debunk these supposed parallels between Jesus and any mini-god. You'll find they are an extended form of hearsay.

For the Egyptian god Horus, for example, you'll find no mention of twelve disciples, three king visitations, death by crucifixion, or a three-day entombment.

3) Ask, *"What do you mean by resurrection?"*

You'll find a significant difference between Jesus' resurrection and what you read in the ancient myths. For example: The Egyptian god Osiris, according to a late tradition recorded in the first century CE by Plutarch, was cut into fourteen pieces by his archenemy, Typhon, who scattered them all along the Nile.

Osiris's wife Isis was able to gather thirteen of those to reassemble her husband. Fish ate the sexual organ, so Isis assembled another out of gold in order for Osiris to impregnate her with Horus. Osiris, since he will never be a complete being again, now resides as the god of the underworld. *How does that line up with the resurrection?*

4) Ask, *"What do you mean by virgin birth?"*

Again, let's use the same example: Given the myth above, calling Horus's conception a virgin birth strains the idea to its breaking point. Another example: Zeus impregnating Semele with Dionysus. He had physical relations with her even though she couldn't see him. Zeus took the fetus and sewed it into his thigh; from there Dionysus was born. *How does that line up with the virgin birth?*

5) Ask, *"Just which calendar were they using?"*

Lastly, the claims of December 25 are completely erroneous. The similarities between Mithraism and Christianity have included their chapels, the term *father* for priest, celibacy, and the December 25 birthdate claims. That last is so widespread that the *Catholic Encyclopedia* entry for "Mithraism" remarks: *"The 25 December was observed as his birthday, the natalis invicti, the rebirth of the winter-sun, unconquered by the rigours of the season."*

As a matter of history, Emperor Aurelian was the first to institute officially the winter solstice as the birthday of *Sol Invictus (Dies Natalis Solis Invicti)* in 274 CE. The first recorded Christmas celebration was in Rome in 336 CE. In 380 CE, Christmas changed from January 6 to December 25.

Many myths don't specify any date at all for the birth of the deities. (Again, read the originals!) But if the Egyptians wanted to be more precise and associate Horus with the solstice, then his birthday would be the December 21 or 22 in the modern calendar, not the 25th.

The *"History of Religions"* hypothesis suggests that the Church selected the December 25 date to connect it to festivities held by the Romans in honor of the sun god, *"Sol Invictus."*

A twelfth-century Syrian bishop, Jacob Bar-Salibi, wrote,

"It was a custom of the Pagans to celebrate on the same 25 December the birthday of the Sun, at which they kindled lights in token of festivity. In these solemnities and revelries the Christians also took part. Accordingly when the doctors of the Church perceived that the Christians has a leaning to this festival, they took counsel and resolved that the true Nativity should be solemnized on that day." (Cited in Christianity and Paganism in the Fourth to Eighth Centuries, Ramsay MacMullen. Yale: 1997, p. 155).

As I've explained, I am not Church bashing, but Jesus' actual birth is not on December 25, and celebrating Christmas then has nothing to do with the winter solstice whatsoever.

THE TEN TOP REASONS TO BELIEVE

(AQ) Questions you ask the Atheist to make him think)

"What is man in nature? Nothing in relation to the infinite, everything in relation to nothing, a mean between nothing and everything" - Blaise Pascal, 1670

EVOLUTION VS CREATION

How do you build a car through evolution? A piece of metal formed from nothing and, through a great deal of time, connected with other pieces of metal, also formed from nothing. Rubber, also formed from nothing, became a certain style (round, with treads).

After billions of years, suddenly a car comes out of this assembly. It is in perfect shape and runs.

IF you believe that, you have more faith than I do. The origin of a car requires processes, like design and manufacturing, that does not exist in nature. We have many cars with different shapes, but they all have one thing in common—a Designer.

How do we know that? They have a design to them. Consider this definition: *"Evolution: Nothing working on nothing by nothing, through nothing, for nothing, beget everything."*

Why is evolution so appealing? It takes God out of the picture. The passage of time and the increase of knowledge have hurt evolution. For evolution to be a FACT, you must have a minimum of two things:

- Life must come from non-life.
- That life must go from simple forms to complex form over time.

Why? You must have a "kickoff" to start the game. If you can't show life coming from non-life, then the game is off.

Life arose on earth by only two choices:

- A series of random events, or
- Creation, either by accident or on purpose.

To answer this choice, we must ask: *Where did the world come from?*

There are two viewpoints and both require faith.

- *"God, the Creator, made it."* This is a logical faith that Intelligent Design carefully made complex things to function together.
- *"Everything that exists now has been formed by accidental random changes to its previous state."* This is the position of the evolutionist, also based on faith.

(AQ) *Which of these two viewpoints is yours? Where is your evidence?*

THE BIG BANG

(See also the chapter: *"Does God Exist? – Evidence from Astronomy."* Let's extend this knowledge) The *"Big Bang"* is an explanation that, with NO Creator, something arose nothing. This is contrary to most basic scientific laws and has no sufficient cause.

The definition of *"THE BIG BANG"* is this: The entire mass of the universe was all in one place, considerably compacted by a tremendous amount of gravity. Then a *"hiccup"* in the nothing, which was already there, produced matter and anti-matter, giving off the energy of the *"BANG."* Here is the problem: This theory is a violation of the laws of conservation of matter and energy.

If the mass were in one place, it would have formed a black hole instead of a universe, unless a tremendous amount of energy could force it apart. The Big Bang model does not give rise to "lumpiness." (If everything was all one particle, how did different atoms arise? Why isn't the universe uniform, instead of having "lumps" of matter (galaxies, stars, planets) scattered about so much empty space?)

The Big Bang's believers criticize creationists as unscientific. *Why?* They believe God, if He exists, caused a violation of the normal running of the natural world when He created. The Big Bang leaves the same miracle—the creation of everything—to occur by the insufficient power of nothing instead of the sufficient power of God. The result is LESS scientific, not MORE.

(AQ) *What, or who, produced the entire mass of the universe in the first place? Was it Quantum Fluctuations or a very intelligent Designer?*

THE LAWS OF NATURE

What produced the "hiccup"? We live in a physical world. Our minds cannot conceive true nothingness. Science has discovered a theology that the Big Bang could have occurred, proving nothing created something.

NASA has a map showing how this could happen. This map shows the beginning of the universe which did not exist that the years ago. It shows the expansion of the universe starting at a single source – Quantum Fluctuations (This map can be found on the Internet at https://www.jpl.nasa.gov/infographics/infographic.view.php?id=10824)

To explain the map two words must be defined: **Inflation** and **Quantum Fluctuations**.

Inflation is the action of inflating something or the condition of being inflated (an example would be the inflation of a balloon)

Quantum Fluctuations is the temporary change in the amount of energy and a point in space.

According to scientists, this has allowed creation of something from nothing provided you had the laws of nature and the law of relativity. Scientists say both were needed to create something from nothing. If that is true, this process does not work. *Why?*

The laws of nature are not physical and cannot operate in nothingness. It can only act on the physical. If it could operate in nothingness it means that they had to preexist the creation of the universe. That's which created the universe is also active in the universe.

We now have a set of forces that are:

1) not physical;

2) are able to act on the physical;

3) create the physical from nothing;

4) predate the universe and our understanding of time; and

5)   still active in the universe.

Sound familiar?

The scientists just described the biblical God who created the heavens — Elohim.

If someone says that a frog turns into a prince, it is a fairy tale. BUT if he adds it took millions of years, people call it "science." Long periods of time suggest that impossible things can happen. When you hear, *"It took millions of years,"* THINK, *"Once upon a time."*

10. THE PROBABILITY OF EVOLUTION

Consider this: The simplest protein molecule contains at least a hundred amino acids. For life to exist, they all must combine in a precise sequence.

Consider this example: In a two-string combination A-B would work, B-A would not. As the number of components increases, the number of possible combinations increases exponentially. One hundred will work out to 10 to the 158th power (1 with 158 zeros). These odds are so high that evolution has no realistic chance for to create life, yet life exists.

(AQ) *Explain how these hundred acids were produced from nothing if there was no designer? Where is your evidence?*

9. EVOLUTION VS THE ORIGIN OF LIFE

The Scientific definition of Life is: "Any organism which is capable of reproducing itself."

Ask yourself this question: *What was the first form of life? Is it a virus, which is the simplest?*

If that is your choice, we have a problem. A virus is a parasite. Its only method of reproduction is by the invasion and destruction of a living cell. No living cell means no reproduction. *What does that mean?* Life could not have begun with a virus; *what would they eat?*

Is it a bacterium, which is the smallest single-cell organism?

We have two types of bacteria.

- Those who live on dead animal or vegetable matter, and

- Those who live on live animal or vegetable matter.

Life could not have begun with bacteria. Again, *if they were the first life form on earth, what would they eat?*

Is it a protozoa, which is the next step up the ladder of life?

We have over 15,000 different species of protozoa, BUT they are also parasites. Again, because they are parasites, *what would they eat?*

What is DNA (Deoxyribonucleic Acid)? It is the detailed blueprint that instructs a cell how to construct an entire organism of ITS OWN KIND. DNA is the language of the genes located on the chromosomes in the cellular nucleus. Because of the duplication and recombining of genes, no offspring will ever be exactly like its parent. Yet it is impossible for any organism to produce an offspring NOT of the species of that organism.

With that in mind, let's take a look at the ameba, a very simple one-celled animal. An ameba reproduces by asexual cell division. One ameba cell divides to produce two individuals in a process called *MITOSIS*, the simplest form of reproduction. The simple mechanism of cell division requires a precise, step-by-step series of EXTREMELY COMPLICATED events.

(AQ) *How did the DNA evolve to master the process of "Mitosis"? How did the ameba survive before this process existed?*

The Problem of Sex

A major problem with evolution is SEX! That's the main difference between the ameba and the higher life forms that supposedly mutated and adapted from it. You only get a limited amount of diversity when a single set of chromosomes splits to create two cells in the place of one. Compare that with the egg-and-sperm reproductive systems of higher life forms.

Based on the theory, sex MUST have been the result of a mutant gene, at precisely the right time in two different individuals of the SAME species (one for male and one for female). For evolution to produce sex, this process would have had to happen in ONE SINGLE GENERATION. Otherwise this mutated individual could not have reproduced itself and passed this characteristic on to its progeny.

(AQ) *Can you produce different explanations to make the appearance of sex work? Where is your evidence?*

Plant-Animal Symbiosis

Let me give you an example: *The Yucca Plant and the Pronuba Moth.*

The yucca plant's natural home is the desert. It has sharp, sword-like leaves and beautiful white flowers. The yucca plant may seem to have mastered its environment perfectly; but its entire existence depends on a moth that hatches in the sand at its roots.

The pronuba moth emerges from a cocoon only on certain nights of the year and it is only on these same nights that the flowers of the yucca plant are in full bloom. The moth follows the fragrance of the flower, enters the flower, and grabs a wad of pollen with its jaws and tentacles. It then flies to another yucca plant flower, enters the flower, jams the pollen deep into the flower, jams a tube through the pollen, and lays its eggs among the seeds of the flower. THEN IT DIES. It lives one night.

While the eggs are incubating, the yucca seeds are ripening. When the eggs hatch, the caterpillar finds a large supply of food. It will eat about one-fifth of the seeds. They then cut a hole in the seed, and spin a silk rope to the desert floor. They then burrow into the sand, build a cocoon, and metamorphose into the moth. So now you may ask: *What is the point?*

(AQ) *The yucca has several varieties, each with a different moth. WHY does the pronuba moth not just lay her eggs in the first flower instead of going through this entire procedure to lay eggs into another flower? How does each different moth know which variety of yucca in which to lay its eggs? Where is your evidence?*

Animal–Animal Symbiosis

An example of this is *The Tarantula and the Tarantula Wasp*.

The tarantula wasp must find, fight, paralyze, and capture a tarantula in order to reproduce. Nothing but a tarantula will do. Any wasp that does not find a tarantula cannot lay her eggs.

(AQ) Consider This: *How did the first tarantula wasp KNOW that its ONE and ONLY means of reproduction was to paralyze a tarantula, drag it to a suitable place, dig a cave, push the spider inside, and lay its eggs on the paralyzed tarantula? How did it know that its larvae would eat nothing BUT the stunned, preserved tarantula?*

The Duckbill Platypus

Let's talk about evolution's nightmare, *The Duckbill Platypus*. It is one of two mammals that lay eggs. Once the eggs hatch, they nurse as any mammal would; but the platypus has no nipples or breast. They lick the hair on the underside of the mother and obtain milk from the hair.

The bill of the platypus is like that of a duck. On each foot are not only five toes, but also webbing. This makes it a cross between a duck and an animal that has to scratch and dig. The external ear is a hole without an ear lobe, which mammals usually have. The platypus is nocturnal. It catches its food under water AND stores worms, snails, and grubs in cheek pouches like the squirrel.

Here is the question: *From WHAT did the platypus evolve?*

- It has the features that resemble the duck and the lizard.

- It has fur like a beaver.

- It lays eggs like a chicken.

- The male platypus has a hollow spur on the inside of its heel, connected to a gland that manufactures venom. (This makes the platypus the only venomous creature with fur)

The platypus needs all this to live perfectly in his environment.

(AQ) *Where did this venomous trait evolve, allowing the platypus to be as poisonous as most deadly snakes? Could "Random Events" have resulted in this unusual combination? Where is your evidence?*

The Caterpillar/Butterfly

If you wanted to invent a life cycle that could never happen by evolution, you would not be able to beat the butterfly. When a butterfly lays an egg, a small butterfly does not hatch, a caterpillar does. Both the caterpillar and the butterfly stages could not have evolved together in a coordinated way at the same time.

(AQ) *Which would most likely evolve first?*

- *A butterfly, with strong light wings designed with the aerodynamics and the nervous system to fly? OR*
- *A caterpillar, which just crawls on the ground?*

If the simple, crawling stage should evolve before the flying stage, we have a MAJOR set of problems:

The caterpillar has protective coloration, often covered with stiff hairs that predators don't like. Butterflies have wings much larger than their bodies, which attract predators. The wings keep them from crawling in the grass like the caterpillar. This makes the caterpillar almost invisible while butterfly, with its brightly colored wings, is a target for predators.

(AQ) *What survival value do big, bright wings have that natural selection should choose them over camouflaged caterpillars?*

Caterpillars chew on vegetation, available most of the year. Butterflies depend on nectar from flowers for substance, reducing the period in which they can eat. Many don't live very long.

(AQ) *WHY would caterpillars, with a strong survival advantage, have evolved into butterflies with survival disadvantages? Where is your evidence?*

The Four Stages of Life

The four stages of the life cycle are *egg, larva* (caterpillar), *pupa*, and *adult* (butterfly).

The caterpillar eats constantly, and then he stops eating and changes into a mummy-like, immobile phase of its life cycle called the pupa. Inside the sac, the organs break down into a liquid soup, from which the wings, legs, eyes, and other structures of the butterfly form. This process is *metamorphosis*.

(AQ) *After the first caterpillar had turned to liquid, could it have waited millions of years to use the liquid to build a beautiful creature that could fly? According to science, how did this process originate for the first time? What are the chances of that? Where is your evidence?*

The caterpillar craws in on six pairs of legs, and after the transformation, he flies off on two pairs of new wings and just three pairs of legs.

The caterpillar goes into the cocoon with a body consisting of thirteen elements. After the transformation, he flies off with a new body of ten elements. The caterpillar has six simple eyes on each side of the head. After the transformation, the butterfly flies off with two compound eyes and one pair of simple eyes.

The caterpillar has short antennae. After the transformation, the butterfly has longer antennae. The caterpillar has no organs for sex or reproduction, but the butterfly does. The caterpillar has strong chewing jaws. After the transformation, the butterfly has a sucking mouth, with a long tube to insert into flowers. This tube coils up when not in use.

The nervous system, organs, muscles and glands of the caterpillar change completely after the transformation. The butterfly gets a complete new nervous system, organs, muscles, and glands necessary to fly and pollinate. The caterpillar has two long and complex glands that exude silk for the cocoon. After the transformation, these glands are gone.

To work under the theory of natural selection, these changes had to offer some survival advantage at EVERY stage.

(AQ) *HOW could all this have happened in a sac of liquid before it rotted? According to science, how could the egg, caterpillar, pupa, and butterfly originate in the first place? Where is your evidence?*

A thinking person who wants to believe in evolution must choose between some very discouraging choices. He can believe:

- The caterpillar evolved first, and then survived without reproductive organs for the millions of generations it took for the butterfly to evolve — the only part of the life cycle capable of sexual reproduction.

How could the caterpillar reproduce during that time?

OR

- The caterpillar evolved first, complete with reproductive organs, but lost them later.

(Isn't this the opposite of the theory of evolution?)

OR

- The more complex flying stage with the sexual organs evolved first, and the simpler crawling stage evolved from it later.

(Again, isn't this the opposite of the theory of evolution?)

OR

- Some completely unknown, super mutation wrote the entire DNA code for all four phases all in one shot, with no necessity for reproductive possibilities until the adult stage.

(Could random mutation reasonably get this exactly right on the first try?)

When a caterpillar enters into the pupa stage, it's like entering a tomb. His body parts decompose into a thick liquid, and Mr. Caterpillar is no more. After a few days, a butterfly comes out and flies off, leaving the last resting place of the caterpillar empty.

Matthew 28:5-6 says, *"And the angel answered and said unto the women, Fear not ye; for I know that ye seek Jesus, who hath been crucified. He is not here; for he is risen, even as he said. Come, see the place where the Lord lay."*

Later, when the Messiah met with Thomas, He made this statement in John 20:28-29: *"Thomas answered and said unto him, 'My Lord and my God.' Jesus saith unto him, 'Because thou hast seen me, thou hast believed: blessed are they that have not seen, and yet have believed.'"*

Some people ask, "Am I suppose to believe that Jesus (Yeshua) rose again, and went flying off into the clouds? How naïve do you think I am?" CONSIDER these people believe that the Messiah COULD NOT, but they believe that the caterpillar COULD.

We can use the caterpillar changing to a butterfly as God's illustration of the fantastic change that takes place in the life of the person who receives New Life in the Messiah.

2 Corinthians 5:17 says, *"Wherefore if any man is in the Messiah, he is a new creature: the old things are passed away; behold, they are become new."*

Just like the caterpillar craws in the dirt of the ground, SO does the man or woman crawl in the dirt of sin and rebellion against God. When the caterpillar enters the pupa stage, the DNA breaks down its body into liquid, then creates a new creature — the Butterfly. Compare that to when you trust in the Messiah — His grace connects and changes you into a beautiful new creature.

The butterfly with its beautiful wings can fly to dimensions the caterpillar never imagined. This also applies when the Ruach Hakodesh (Holy Spirit) enters your life. It places you into a spiritual dimension and lets you fly to spiritual heights and fellowship with God Himself. *WHY crawl, when by God's help you can fly?*

There is about as much evolutionary evidence that caterpillars evolved into butterflies as there is for the horse evolving into a Model-T Ford.

1 John 2:20-21 (JNT) says, *"But you have received the Messiah's anointing from HaKadosh, and you know all this. It is not because you don't know the truth that I have written to you, but because you do know it, and because no lies has its origin in the truth."*

The Human Body

Is the human body a design or is it by chance?

- The **brain** has ten million nerve cells to record what you see and hear. *By chance?*

- The **skin** has over two million (3000 per square inch) tiny sweat glands. *By chance?*

- The **heart** pumps the blood over 168 million miles a day. This is equal to 6720 times around the earth. *By chance?*

- The **lining of the stomach** contains 35 million glands, secreting juices that aid in digestion. *By chance?*

(AQ) *Was the body a design or was it by chance? If by chance, how much time did evolution need to produce just these four parts of the human body? According to science, how did the human body survive within that time period? Where is your evidence?*

Why is the belief in human evolution SO DANGEROUS? This thinking helped to produce the Holocaust—HOW?

If you were an accident, you have no destiny or purpose in life, and you have no value. You're just a pawn in a cosmic game of chance. Remember, Hitler ("Man of the Year" in 1938) was an evolutionist. He used "survival of the fittest" to present the Jewish people as something rejected by God and nature. Therefore, their extermination would be necessary to make room on earth for the "superior race."

The Universe

Let's consider the universe. *Does the universe have a Designer, or is it by chance?*

Hebrews 11:3 says, *"By Faith we understand that the worlds were prepared by the word of God so that what is seen was not made out of things which are visible"* (NASB).

Science says that nothing created something out of nothing. *Who really has "blind faith"?*

Matter holds together by natural charges. The nucleus of an atom contains positively charged protons that should repel each other; yet they don't fly apart. An equal number of electrons in the outer shell balances their repulsive force — but how did they get into this stable configuration? The electrons ought to repel each other too! How could you bring positive protons and negative electrons together and not have them immediately attract each other to form hydrogen atoms?

Consider this answer: Colossians 1:16-17 says, *"For by Him all things were created, both in the heavens and on earth, visible and invisible, whether thrones or dominions, or rulers or authorities – all things have been created by Him and for Him. And He is before all things, and in Him all things hold together"* (NASB).

By Jesus, all things hold together.

The earth is small compared to other planets. Consider this:

- You can take 1,300,300 Earths and place them inside our sun.

- Some stars are bigger than our sun. The star Antares can have 64 of our suns placed in it.

- There is another star in the Hercules constellation, Alpha Herculis, which can hold a million of the star Antares. (That is not the biggest star.)

- The star Epsilon can hold four million of that star.

NOW READ Psalm 8:3-4, *"When I consider Thy heavens, the work of Thy fingers, the moon and the stars, which Thou hath ordained. What is man that Thou dost take thought of him? And the son of man that Thou dost care for him"* (NASB)?

DO you have any idea how big your God is? Read Jeremiah 32:17, *"Is there anything too hard for Me?"*

Look at the way the disciples prayed in Acts 4:24 — *"And when they heard this, they lifted their voices to God with one accord and said, 'O Lord, it is Thou who DIDST MAKE THE HEAVENS AND THE EARTH AND THE SEA and all that is in them'"* (NASB).

They recognized God as Creator then made their request. Evolution is NOT scientific if it rejects God. You cannot find the right answer if you remove the possibility of

God prior to examining the physical evidenced. *If evolution is not science, what is it?* It is philosophy.

8. EVOLUTION OVERTURNED BY GENETICS

According to evolution, life began as simple forms and over long periods of time became increasingly complex. The meaning of *Complex* is *"having a large number of component parts."*

Let's apply an example of modern genetics — chromosomes. If life has become increasingly complex, we would expect to find a growing number of chromosomes in more advanced organisms. *Is that what we get?* Let's look at a few examples:

- Corn   = 20 Chromosomes.
- Mouse   = 40 Chromosomes.
- Human   = 46 Chromosomes (so far, so good.)
- Potato   = 48 Chromosomes.

This presents only two choices:

- Either evolution is true, and a potato is more advanced than a human,

OR

- Chromosomes indicate that life is not on an upward spiral.

(AQ) *What is your choice? (Remember: If you choose number two, you yourself have destroyed evolution.) How did the chromosomes originate? Where is your evidence?*

7. UNITY IN THE TANAKH

We must understand three things when dealing with Scriptures.

1. In today's courts, diaries are admissible as testimony and evidence. All critics of ancient manuscripts still follow Aristotle's *Dictum*, which states, "The benefit of the doubt is to be given to the document itself, not arrogated by the critic to himself."

2. Unless the document exhibits internal contradictions or factual inaccuracies (i.e. the Eiffel Tower is in London), we presume the document is true, and the burden is on the critic to prove otherwise.

3. You do not argue from silence. Just because we have never found an extra-Biblical reference that does not mean it didn't happen. Critics argued for 150 years against the existence of Pontius Pilate...until in 1947, an archaeologist uncovered a stile with his name on it.

Nevertheless, new critics look other items that have their sole reference in the Biblical account.

The Old Testament (Tanakh)

As mentioned previously ("Is the Bible True?"), the Tanakh took numerous generations to write over about a thousand years. It contains 39 books written by dozens of authors, ranging from peasants and shepherds to scholars, priests, and kings. Because of the scope of time and authorship, any numerical unity would be impossible to coordinate.

Consider this example of numerical unity: We have also mentioned how the number seven represents God's divine perfection, completeness, and order. Let's see how it is connected, through mathematics, to Scripture.

- The number seven appears 287 times (41 x 7).

- The word *seventh* appears 98 times (14 x 7).

- The number *seventy* appears 56 times (8 x 7).

- The word *sevenfold* has seven appearances.

These multiples of seven are astonishing. They show a higher intelligence behind the text.

(AQ) *Can you prove these multiples were accidental? How? Where is your evidence?*

6. ARCHEOLOGY CONFIRMS THE SCRIPTURES

Here is an example of archaeology confirming Scripture: We learn about the walls of Jericho in Joshua 6:20 — *"So the people shouted, and the priests blew the trumpets; and it came to pass, when the people heard the sound of the trumpet, that the people shouted with a great shout, and* **the wall fell down flat,** *so that the people went up into the city, every man straight before him, and they took the city."*

There are three ways a wall can fall:

- *Straight down,* which would create huge piles of rubble (typical of an earthquake).

- *Inward.* Most Middle East excavations reveal inward falls, mainly due to invading armies pressing in from the outside. This creates obstacles when the walls land on buildings.

- *Outward.* Only by falling outward could the walls end up flat, allowing everyone to enter straight in.

With this information in mind, consider this fact: In 1929, Dr J.B. Garstang led an archeological expedition to Jericho. After an extensive dig, he discovered that the walls had actually fallen outward. This discovery is tangible proof of an extraordinary event.

Let's look at a second EXAMPLE: Genesis 1:2 says, *"And the earth was waste and void; and darkness was upon the face of the deep: and the Spirit of God moved upon the face of the waters."*

Scholars believed the word *TEHOM* ("*the deep*") in Genesis 1:2 was a late word, demonstrating the late writing of the Creation story. However, this word appeared on clay tablets discovered in 1970 in Ebla, in northern Syria. The age of the tablets indicated the word was in use some eight hundred years before Moses.

Here is an third EXAMPLE: Isaiah 20:1 says, *"In the year that Tartan came unto Ashdod, when Sargon the king of Assyria sent him, and he fought against Ashdod and took it;"*

Critics once claimed Assyrian had no king named *Sargon* because Isaiah had the only record of this name. That was until the discovery of Sargon's Palace in Iraq. Moreover, on the palace walls recorded his capture of Ashdod — the very event mentioned in Isaiah 20.

Here is an fourth EXAMPLE: Daniel 5:16 says, *"But I have heard of thee, that thou canst give interpretations, and dissolve doubts; now if thou canst read the writing, and make known to me the interpretation thereof, thou shalt be clothed with purple, and have a chain of gold about thy neck, and* **shalt be the third ruler in the kingdom.***"*

Another king in doubt was Daniel's Belshazzar, King of Babylon. The last recorded king was Nabonidus until archaeologists found tablets showing that Belshazzar was Nabonidus's son and co-regent in Babylon. *What does this mean?*

Balshazzar's position allowed him the authority to make Daniel *"third highest ruler in the Kingdom."* This agrees perfectly with the Bible account.

(AQ) *Do you know of an example that shows Archaeology disagreeing with scripture? Where is your evidence? (Remember rule #3: "You do not argue from silence")*

5. ARCHITECTURE SUPPORTS THE SCRIPTURES

Out of many, let's look at this EXAMPLE: 1 Kings 9:15 says, *"And this is the reason of the levy which king Solomon raised, to build the house of Adonai, and his own house, and Millo, and the wall of Jerusalem, and* **Hazor, and Megiddo**, *and Gezer."*

It attributes both of these cities, Hazor and Megiddo, to a single construction tax. This shows a strong indication of an intimate or close relationship. In 1960, an expedition led by Yadin excavated Megiddo. Among the findings was an exact design of the city gate, consisting of three chambers on each side. Prior to the dig of Hazor, Yadin instructed his team to trace Megiddo's layout on top of the Hazor site.

By carefully aligning their measurements, they pinpointed the precise location where the gate would appear. They discovered the identical gate, with three chambers on each side, in the exact spot as the Megiddo dimensions. This proved that not only Solomon built both gates, but that both had followed a single master plan.

(AQ) *Do you know of an example that shows Architecture disagreeing with scripture? Where is your evidence?*

4. ASTRONOMY VINDICATES THE SCRIPTURES

Consider this EXAMPLE: Jeremiah 33:22 (AMP) says, *"As the host of (the stars of) the heavens cannot be numbered, not the sand of the sea be measured, so I will multiply the offspring of David My servant, and the Levites who minister to Me."*

In Jeremiah's day, this verse seemed ridiculous. Only a few hundred stars were visible to the naked eye. In 100 CE, Ptolemy could only catalogue about a thousand stars. In 1642, Galileo increased the grand total to around three thousand. For 26 centuries, the scriptures seemed in error based on this verse. However, modern telescopes have proved it correct. Today, astronomers estimate trillions of stars in the heavens.

(AQ) *Do you know of an example that shows astronomy disagreeing with scripture? Where is your evidence?*

3. THE LITERAL FULFILLMENT OF PROPHECY

We have discussed the fulfillment of prophecies, but in this section, I will give two additional examples:

EXAMPLE #1: Psalm 22:16 describes crucifixion. It is one of many such passages. You must be understand two things about the context when the passage was written.

- This Psalm appeared hundreds of years before the time of the Messiah.

- This Psalm had the cultural context of the ancient Hebrew nation.

To a nation that exclusively used stoning for capital punishment, death by crucifixion was an unknown practice. It probably originated with the Assyrians and Babylonians. Since the psalmist could not have known about this method of punishment, we have to ask, *"HOW could he have written such an amazingly accurate prophecy unless inspired by God to do so?"*

EXAMPLE #2: Read Daniel 2:30-45. It is Interpretation of Nebuchadnezzar's dream. Now, consider this: Daniel lived from 605 BCE to 536 BCE. During his time, the Babylon Empire fell in 556 BCE. Then the Medes and Persians (CHALDEAN?) Empire ruled until 539 BCE.

The Persian Empire lasted from 539 BCE to 331 BCE, followed by the Greek Empire from 331 BCE to 58 BCE. The last empire, founded in 756 BCE, was the Roman Empire from 58 BCE to 476 CE.

Daniel had no idea of this history when he interpreted Nebuchadnezzar' dream. As mentioned before in this book, how do you know a prophecy is true? If someone says it is going to happen, and it happens, than the prophecy is true. Such was the case of Daniel.

(AQ) *Do you know an example of prophecy in Scripture that you can prove wrong? Where is your evidence? (Remember: you do not argue from silence.)*

2. MODERN SCIENCE VERIFIES THE SCRIPTURES

Isaiah 40:22, written around 600 BCE, says, *"It is he that sitteth above the **circle of the earth**, and the inhabitants thereof are as grasshoppers; that stretcheth out the heavens as a curtain, and spreadeth them out as a tent to dwell in;"*

At a time when many believed the earth was flat—and, depending on your culture, possibly resting on the back of a giant turtle—this verse recognizes that the earth is a circle—round.

Let's look at another scripture. Job is considered the oldest book of the Bible, written about 1500 BCE. Job 26:7 says, *"He stretches out the north over empty space, **and hangs the earth upon nothing**."*

This is a clear picture of earth suspended in space—common knowledge today, but hardly apparent from the ground. *Could the Scriptures be more correct?*

(AQ) *What fact, not theory, in modern science disagrees with Scripture? Where is your evidence?*

1. THE PROPHETIC AND SCIENTIFIC ACCURACY OF THE MESSIAH

You judge a prophet by the fulfillment of His prophecy. Jesus perfectly prophesied the destruction of Jerusalem by Roman troops. This happened just as He said in 70 CE! Jesus also prophesied that the Jewish people would scatter to the far reaches of the earth, and this happened. Again, Jesus prophesied they would gathered together again in the last days. This happened in 1948 with the establishment of the nation of Israel.

Yet again, Jesus prophesied that Jerusalem would break free from the *"heel of the Gentile,"* and this happened during the 1967 War. For the first time since 70 CE, Jerusalem was again under Jewish rule.

Remember, the chapter "Is the Bible True?" numbered at least 454 prophecies, twenty in one 24-hour period, that was fulfilled by one , Messiah Ben Joseph. Messiah Ben David will fulfill the rest.

Again, I say, *"If someone says it is going to happen, and it happens, than the prophecy is true."*

(AQ) If you disagree with this statement, then answer this question: "What is Truth?"

DNA & REPRODUCTION

The DNA tells the cell what it should do and gives the specific information necessary for making the complex proteins comprising the cell so it can do its job. *Could DNA, the world's most efficient carrier and user of information have arisen by CHANCE?*

It doesn't matter if the information in the cell is written on DNA, RNA, clay tablets, or a blackboard. The question is *WHERE DID THE INFORMATION COME FROM?*

Some people may ask: *Can't anything happen if you give it enough time?* Since time does not PRODUCE information, more time would NOT produce more information. It is like asking, *"How long would my car motor have to run to produce an elephant?"*

(AQ) *How did the DNA code originate? Can you prove, through science, that chance produced advanced life without the process of DNA? Where is your evidence?*

What if the first living cell formed without its DNA already programmed to reproduce? Then all life would be over the moment it died! If life arose from NON-LIVING molecules, what is the chance that <u>ON THE FIRST TRY</u> it would have the program to produce copies of itself? It would have been an achievement worthy of a God much more powerful than *"a bit more time."*

(AQ) *Again, can you process that chance produced life without the process of DNA? How does the DNA evolve naturally to change one species to another different species? Again, where is your evidence?*

Evolutionists now theorize that life may have come to earth from another planet by a meteor or a comet. So life must have evolved out in space somewhere because they realize that it couldn't have happened under the laws of science on earth. Think of it as saying, *"Once upon a time in a land far, far away."*

CONCLUSION

At the very beginning of the chapter of the battleground *"Does God Exist,"* we placed you into a jury. I am going to close this book with the questions mentioned at the beginning.

- *How much evidence would you require to convict or acquit?*

- *Would you convict on circumstantial evidence only or would you want as much evidence as you can get?*

- *Would you want that evidence to come from only one source or from many sources?*

Another two questions:

- *Have we presented only circumstantial evidence or have we presented facts that can be tracked, studied, and tested by many sources?*

- *Have your answers given you any cause to rethink your position?*

I would like close this book by ask another question. *What if you thought something was true, and you found out it was wrong, when would you want to know it?*

Dan Cain, in his small 23 page book, *"8 Absurd Things Atheists Must Believe Before Breakfast,"* gave one of the best examples of what remains when God is taken out of the picture.

The consequences are:

- No meaning in life;
- No value in life;
- No significance in life;
- No purpose in life;
- No hope in life, and the last one;
- Some may think there are no restraints against evil impulses.

When I was an atheist, this was my life. *"Is it yours?"*

Here is the final point to consider: If you can believe Genesis 1:1, you will have NO PROBLEM with the rest of the Bible. Jonah and the whale, an ax head that floats, a virgin birth, Jesus walking on water, the Red Sea parting, the Resurrection, and miracles will seem commonplace.

Genesis 1:1 reads, *"In the beginning God created the heaven and the earth."*

If you cannot believe that, you will question the rest; but the final question you must answer is *"What If I'm Wrong."*

APPENDICES

BIBLES AND THEIR FUNCTIONS

You may misuse Scripture when you:

1. are ignorant about what it says on a given subject
2. take a verse out of its context
3. read your own meaning into a passage and make it say what it does not
4. give undue emphasis to less important things
5. use it to try to get God to do what you want, rather than what God wants done

Have you ever gone to a Bible study where someone responds to a verse with, "That is not how it is reads in my Bible"?

What happens?

The Bible study dissolves into a discussion on which Bible version is correct (we'll assume nobody has authored their own). This places a lack of trust in the word of God.

Knowledge can correct this problem.

What Bible should you use? It depends on this: What is your purpose or function?

Why?

"**To translate is to destroy.**" You CANNOT use one kind of Bible and expect it to fulfill the purpose of another. These five bible types are:

Word for Word (literal, complete equivalent): This type attempts to translate by keeping as close as possible to the exact words and phrasing in the original language, yet still making sense in the translated language. A literal translation will keep the historical portion intact at all points

Thought for Thought (Dynamic Equivalent): This type attempts to translate the words, idioms, and grammatical constructions of the original language into equivalents in the translated language. This type of translation keeps the historical distance on all historical and MOST factual matters, but "updates" matters of language, grammar, and style. You should NOT use this to determine the meanings of words.

Paraphrase-free: This type attempts to translate the ideas from one language to another with less concern about using the exact words of the original. It tries to eliminate as much of the historical distance as possible for an "easy read."

Theologically biased: This type will "line up" with the teaching or doctrines of a particular group or belief. It can mistranslate words, historical context, and culture to "fit" the doctrines or beliefs.

Culturally biased: This is like the previous one, except it will "Line Up" with a particular race or culture.

With these functions in mind, let's look at some of the Bibles.

Word for Word:

- King James Bible (KJ)
- New King James (NKJ)
- New American Standard Bible (NASB)
- New Revised Standard Version (NRSV)
- Revised Standard Version (RSV)

Thought for Thought:

- New International Version (NIV)
- Today's English Version (TEV)
- Contemporary English Version (CEV)
- New Living Translation (NLT)
- Good News Bible (GNB)
- Jerusalem Bible (JB)
- New English Bible (NEB)

Paraphrase:

- The Living Bible (LB)
- The Message

- Phillips Bible

Theologically Biased:
- Jehovah Witness's New World Translation
- The Amplified Bible (AMP)
- Restoration of the Original Sacred Name Bible
- The Book of Yahweh
- Sacred Scriptures
- Holy Name Bible
- Exegeses Ready Research Bible
- Joseph Smith Translation

Culturally Biased:
- Complete Jewish Bible (CJB)
- Orthodox Jewish Bible (OJB)
- La Biblia de las Americas (Espanol) (BLA)

This list is by no means complete, but by knowing the functions of the Bibles, you can settle some disputes between people who study Scripture.

It also corrects another problem: When the wrong kind of Bible, such as a "Theologically Biased" Bible for a "Word for Word" function, it does not work

I personally use the "Hebrew and Greek Study Bible," written in the format of the New American Standard Bible, giving it the "Word for Word" function.

This Bible also allows me to look up the words against their meaning in Greek and Hebrew within the Bible itself.

PaRDeS - SCRIPTURE THROUGH THE JEWISH LENS

When you study Scripture through the Jewish lens, you have four levels of the interpretation of Scripture (PaRDeS):

1) **Parshat**–Literal, simple plain intended meaning
2) **Remez**–Alluded meaning "reading between the lines"
3) **D'rash**–drawn-out meaning (Midrash – "concept")
4) **Sod**–Hidden meaning

These four levels were in use at the time of Jesus and Paul. Judaism still use them today.

Parshat

The Parshat is the literal, plain meaning of the scripture in its context. Under no conditions must this level be destroyed. If you use a "Remez," "D'rash," or "Sod" interpretation process that changes the context of the Parshat, you are taking a scripture out of its context.

Remez

Remez places an event, process, or scripture into something else and produces a different understanding.

An example of Remez is Gematria (word-number values).

Another example would be Proverbs 20:10—"Different weights, and different measures, both of them are alike an abomination to the Lord."

Matthew used this process when he quoted Hosea in Matthew 2:15—*"Out of Egypt I called My Son."*

How?

When you read the original in Hosea 11:1, you will see that statement applying to Israel.

Matthew is using a Remez to show that the Messiah represents Israel.

The Jewish anti-missionaries will use the Literal (Parshat), and you will apply the Remez. Both are correct. It is not either/or, but both/and (different understanding).

Another example would be when the scripture says, *"The Kingdom of Heaven is like…"*

The Kingdom of Heaven is like …

- A king who wanted to settle accounts with His servants
- A farmer who scattered seed on the ground
- A mustard seed
- A man who planted good seed in his field

- Leaven that a woman placed in a large amount of dough
- Treasure a man found in a field
- A merchant who was searching for fine pearls
- A fishing net thrown in the sea that gathers fish of every kind
- A homeowner who brings out new and old treasures
- A landowner who hired workers for his vineyard
- A king who gave a great banquet
- Ten virgins who took their lamps to meet the Groom
- An employer who gave talents to his servants to invest

Problem: you cannot use this process to take a scripture to produce a doctrine that violates the Scripture. (the Church being 'New Israel')

In history, Origin misused this process to help produce the doctrines of the Constantine Church.

D'rash:

The D'rash is a drawn-out meaning. Or a interpretative meaning. It can come from a life application of a Midrash ("concept"), or a sermon.

An example is in Matthew 18:18, *"Whatever you bind on earth will be bound in heaven, and whatever you loose on earth will be loosed in heaven."*

It is a concept concerning the decisions you make in your personal "walk with God" (*halakha*).

Sod

The Sod (meaning "secret") stays hidden until it becomes public through the Ruach Hakodesh (Holy Spirit). (You will love this example.)

Question: Where in scripture does it say that the WORD is the Messiah? You will find it in John 1:1-2. It does not exist, in the Parshat sense, in the Old Testament.

Jewish anti-missionaries will be quick to mention this. How can the WORD be a Person?

Here is the answer: During the time of Jesus, the Jewish people spoke three languages: Hebrew, Greek, and Aramaic (Aramaic is close to Hebrew and the main language of the common Jew).

With this in mind, let's look at the meanings of *WORD*: Devar (Hebrew) — A word given in action. (The Torah is the "action word of God") Logos, Rhama (Greek)

- Logos — A general word of information
- Rhama — A general word as it applies to you

Memra (Aramaic) — A divine person. (It used in the Aramaic Targums, the Aramaic translations of the Torah and the Old Testament. They were translated about 100 BCE.)

When John wrote his verses in John 1:1-2 in Greek, he used the Greek word logos and connected it to the Word used in creation (Hebrew) but he was applying the Aramaic understanding (*Memra*) to his verses.

If he had not done it, both the Jews (Hebrews) and the Greeks would have rejected the verses.

THE POWER AND SECURITY OF PSALM 91

Question: What is God's Shadow? Psalm 91 mentions *"God's shadow,"* but James 1:17 says God has no shadow.

I believe "God's shadow" is the power (anointing) of God. Psalm 91, written by Moses, tells about the protection given to believers who *"dwell in the secret place."* I believe that "secret place" is Bible study and prayer. Because of what Jesus has done, Bible study and prayer equals fellowship with God.

If I were to outline the 91st Psalm, it would be in three sections:

I.   The conditions;

II. Who is doing the protection;

III. The extent of that protection.

We have discussed the conditions (Bible study and prayer), but who is the protector? All of God's glory is represented by His Name. FOUR Names of God appear in verses 1 and 2.

They are:

1) "The Most High" which, in Hebrew, is "Elyone," meaning "Lofty and Supreme."

2) "Almighty" in Hebrew is "SHADDAI," meaning "The Strong and Mighty One."

3) "Lord," which, in Hebrew, is not pronounced by the Jewish people; but is called "HaShem" or "The Name." This is the "I AM" given to Moses at the burning bush. One of the meanings is, "I will be with you wherever you go."

4) "God," which in Hebrew is "Elohim," the Creator who made the world from nothing and the Supreme God of Israel.

How would you like to have Him on your side as your protector?

Next Question: What is the extent of that protection? Please open your Bible to Psalm 91 and allow the anointing of God to give understanding.

From verse 3 to verse 16, it gives you the Power of God's deliverance and protection. It informs you, in verse 5, that you will receive protection from some attacks unawares.

In verse 7, I believe that the ones who fall on your right and left sides are not your enemies, because you normally face, or run from, them. Rather, they are other believers who did not fulfill the conditions of verses 1 and 2. Verse 13, I believe, talks about protection from the enemies of your soul.

The most powerful verses in this Psalm are verses 14-16. The personal noun of these verses changes from "He" to "I." God, Himself, is speaking through the mouth of Moses. The extent of God's protection is awesome!

Consider this: You are ...

A. Protected from your front by verses 3, 4, 5 & 9;

B. Protected from your back by verses 3, 5 & 9;

C. Protected on your right side by verses 3, 7 & 9;

D. Protected on your left side by verses 3, 7 & 9;

E. Protected from your top by verses 3, 4, 5 & 9;

F. Protected from your bottom by verses 3, 4, 9 & 13;

G. Protected during the day by verses 3, 5, 6 & 9

H. Protected during the night by verses 3, 5, 6 & 9

I. Protected inside your home by verses 3, 9 & 10;

J. Protected outside your home by verses 3, 10 & 14;

K. Protected in this life by verses 8, 11, 15 & 16; and

L. Protected in the life to come by verse 16

Indeed, God's protection is awesome!